Focus on Hinduism
and Buddhism

Robert A. McDermott
Series Editor

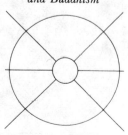

Ordination Procession

Buddhism and Society in Southeast Asia

Donald K. Swearer

ANIMA BOOKS, 1981

Swearer, Donald K.
Buddhism and society in southeast Asia.

Bibliography: p.
1. Sociology, Buddhist—Asia, Southeastern. 2. Buddhism—Asia, Southeastern. 3. Buddhism—Asia, Southeastern—Audio-visual aids—Catalogs. I. Title.
BQ410.S93 294.3'37 81-8048
ISBN 0-89012-023-4 (pbk.) AACR2

This volume is part of a series of guides for the audio-visual materials useful for the study of Hinduism and Buddhism. Preparation and publication were made possible by a grant from the National Endowment for the Humanities to the Council on International and Public Affairs, Inc. (Ward Morehouse, President), with Robert A. McDermott as Project Director. Through the Endowment's provision for matching funds, this project was supported by the Ada Howe Kent Foundation and Baruch College, CUNY.

Printed in USA.

ANIMA BOOKS is a subdivision of Conococheague Associates, Inc., 1053 Wilson Avenue, Chambersburg, Pennsylvania 17201.

Foreword

AS WITH the authors of other volumes in this series,* the author of this essay-guide, Dr. Donald K. Swearer, combines a scholar's knowledge of Asian religion and a thorough familiarity with the audio-visual materials useful for college level study. This guide, and the other publications generated by the same project,† is part of an effort to help professors and students who are left at a disadvantage by the imbalance between the advanced level of scholarship on Asian religions and the rather elementary stage of work on audio-visual materials.

It is from the vantage point of textual and historical scholarship, linguistic fluency and personal experience in Thailand that Professor Swearer contends that Buddhism in Southeast Asia must be seen to be understood. This guide also assumes, however, that seeing is itself a difficult task, and requires the kind of background knowledge provided in Professor Swearer's essay. This essay should be read for the social and political context which makes more intelligible audio-visual treatments of Buddhist practice in this part of the world.

In his essay, Professor Swearer presents Theravāda Buddhism in Sri Lanka and Southeast Asia from the perspective of three socio-political contexts: 1) the first chapter treats traditional Buddhism in the context of the village and small town. Professor Swearer explains, and shows examples of, two significant processes, integration and syncretism. More specifically, this chapter offers vivid accounts of master stories and paradigmatic models, as well as two festivals and two rites of passage, as ways of showing the syncretic nature of popular Buddhism and its integrative function in the daily lives of its adherents in Southeast Asia. 2) In the second chapter, Professor Swearer discusses the relationship between Buddhist teaching and four significant political models: a) The Buddha as one who establishes and sustains the ideal order of the world; b) Devarājā (God-King, or divinized ruler) particularly as memorialized in monumental creations such as Borobudur, Angkor and Pagan; c) King Aśoka (B.C. 270-232), the Exemplary Buddhist Ruler; d) examples of modern

*See Harry M. Buck, *Spiritual Discipline in Hinduism, Buddhism and the West*; Diana Eck, *Darśana: The Visual in the Hindu Religious Tradition*; Richard B. Pilgrim, *Buddhism and the Arts of Japan*.

†See *Focus on Buddhism,* a comprehensive critical guide to the films, slide sets and recordings useful for the study of Buddhism; Professor Swearer is the primary author of the reviews of Southeast Asian or Theravāda materials. A companion volume, *Focus on Hinduism*, is also available.

Buddhist political leaders (specifically, U Nu of Burma and S.W.R.D. Bandaranaike of Sri Lanka). 3) Finally, the third chapter examines the response of traditional Buddhism, as viewed through the respective roles of the monk and the laity, to the challenges of modernization and social transformation.

While Professor Swearer's essay stands on its own as an introduction to Buddhism in the context of Southeast Asian social and political institutions, it gains in richness when complemented by one or more of the films recommended in the section on audio-visual resources. Similarly, while the several films recommended can be used independent of the essay, all of these films will be more effective when seen in the light of the background provided by the social and political analyses provided in Professor Swearer's essay. In addition to the essay and guide to audio-visual resources, this volume includes extensive notes, a bibliography of works on Buddhism in Southeast Asia, and a glossary of terms found in the essay and in some of the films.

Robert A. McDermott
Series Editor

To

SUSAN AND STEPHEN

Who taught me the value of the

visual when discussing religion

Map from Milton Osborne, *Southeast Asia: An Introductory History*
(London: George Allen & Unwin, 1979). Used with permission.

Contents

Preface

THIS VOLUME has been part of an ambitious project funded by the National Endowment for the Humanities which has sought to develop materials for the identification and use of audio-visual materials in the instruction of Asian religions. I have been honored to be a part of the project, and have been educated in the subject matter as one of the participants. In the process friendships with peers and colleagues have deepened, and I have come to appreciate anew their expertise. I am particularly grateful to Bob McDermott who, as the project director, had to spend his time untying administrative and bureaucratic knots, and to David Dell the project coordinator. Others from whom I learned and benefitted were Bob Thurman, Fred Streng, John Carter, Dan Smith, and especially Dick Pilgrim with whom I collaborated on the third stage of the project. Eugene B. Bruns, chairman of the Southeast Asian Studies division of the Foreign Service Institute, deserves thanks for the opportunity he provided me to develop many of these ideas in lectures at the Institute.

Finally, it should be mentioned that the audio-visual references throughout this essay are fully identified and reviewed in *Focus on Buddhism*. Several of the major films on Theravāda Buddhism are discussed in the concluding section on Audio-Visual Resources.

Donald K. Swearer

Swarthmore College
August, 1980

Introduction

A. The Study of Religion and Audio-Visual Instructional Materials

EVERYONE RECOGNIZES the saying, "It has to be *seen* to be *believed*." With one rather modest change – "it has to be *seen* to be *understood*" – this familiar quip becomes peculiarly appropriate to the study of religion. An essay on Buddhism and society in Southeast Asia and the relevant role of audio-visual instructional materials might appropriately begin with a few reflections on this claim. In particular, to be *seen* in order to be *understood* entails two essentially interrelated components: complexity and multivalency.

A religious system consists of a wide diversity of phenomena, e.g., sacred texts, myths, symbols, institutions, rites, and rituals. A religion encompasses even more than a stipulated set of beliefs and practices, however; it also embodies and expresses the genius of a particular culture. Because of this diversity and complexity religion cannot be easily comprehended in any holistic sense. The study of a religious system or even of specific aspects of that system, therefore, calls for analytical and discursive skills, literary imagination, and perceptual acuity. In sum, the nature of the phenomena constituting a religious system cannot be adequately understood by a univocal epistemology or by a single methodology.

To be sure, one course in religion or a particular religious tradition must set reasonable limits as to what it can accomplish. Regardless of its focus, however, any single course that does not take into account the richness and diversity constituting its broader context runs the risks of reductionism and blatant distortion. The New Testament, for example, should certainly be studied from historical and literary critical perspectives, however, as Wilfred C. Smith has suggested,[1] it should also be understood as a sacred scripture which has influenced lives and shaped perceptions throughout a 2000-year history. From this broad point of view one could argue that a New Testament course in historical or literary methodology might be important in the development of exegetical skills, but that it fails as a study of sacred scripture in the sense suggested by Professor Smith. To be even more argumentative, one might claim that such a course teaches a particular kind of exegesis but it is really not a course in religion. By this kind of provocation I do not intend to stipulate the best way to study the New Testament, but simply to suggest that a historical-critical methodology by itself is not adequate to understand the nature and role of the New Testament as a sacred scripture within the lives of Christians and the history of the Christian tradition. To understand the New Testament in this latter sense calls for a "seeing," a more complete or total form of awareness, a knowing not limited to the analytical or even the conceptual.

The difficulty of understanding a religious tradition in its variety and complexity becomes even more acute for non-Western religions. Some of the assumptions operable in our study of Christianity or Judaism may not be as relevant in our study of Hinduism or Buddhism. Some may be entirely irrelevant. And, while our cultural background and general education have provided us with a kind of introduction to Western religious concepts, history, and institutions, we have little such preparation when it comes to non-Western religions. This problem demands that we utilize a wide variety of instructional resources. In the first instance, undoubtedly, these resources will be texts and monographs. In the field of Theravāda Buddhism in Southeast Asia such materials range over primary texts in original languages and in translation, historical studies, doctrinal expositions, and an increasing number of excellent anthropological studies. Although the breadth of available written sources makes possible a more holistic presentation of Theravāda Buddhism in Southeast Asia, the cultural and institutional dimensions remain only relatively accessible without the use of audio-visual resources. For example, we can verbally describe an ordination ceremony or a *pūjā*; however, visual depiction both compliments what may be a relatively interesting ethnographic description and enhances the meaning attributed through the conceptual understanding of such rites.[2] In another context I have taken a similar position in regard to religious practices such as meditation,[3] namely, that actual participation in *vipassanā* meditation or *zazen* illuminates our understanding of this kind of religious practice. The same sort of claim could be made for participation in festivals, rites, and rituals. My argument here rests on epistemological and methodological grounds and has nothing to do with the position that to understand Buddhism one must be a professing Buddhist, or to understand Christianity one must be a baptized member of a church. Quite simply, if a religious phenomenon is most adequately comprehended by accounting for its multiple meanings, our methods of understanding and teaching the phenomena that constitute religion should be appropriate to the nature of the subject matter.

Religions are multiplex, and the phenomena constituting religion embody different levels of meaning. Given this multivalency of meaning religion has been characterized as a "symbol system."[4] To study and teach religion, therefore, challenges us to go beyond the literal, the obvious, and the purely descriptive, to discern the hidden meanings and deeper levels of human experience embedded in the text, the rite, and the festival. To fail to do so may be to ignore the "essence" of a religious symbol system in the face of its myriad "manifestations."[5]

Audio-visual instructional materials contribute to a more complete and, hence, more profound understanding of many religious phenomena.

The saying, "A picture is worth a thousand words," suggests that it takes a lot of words to convey what a picture (or a film or a record) can tell us. A picture, however, can convey more than can be quantified in a thousand or even two thousand words. The student can read descriptions and analyses of funerals or ordinations, but seeing them — even on film — directly involves the perceptual senses in the learning process. In the hands of a well informed and skillful teacher, therefore, appropriate audio-visual instructional materials help provide a more complete understanding of religion. Films, slides, records, tapes, artifacts, ritual utensils, and so on, need to be integrated into interpretative frameworks. By themselves their variety of meanings may remain mute; however, without them the study of religion may become overly conceptual and in doing so run the risk of distorting the fundamental nature of the subject matter.

B. Aim of this Essay

Not so many years ago religion courses were often taught in philosophy or literature departments. Although historical reasons account for such department loci, these identifications point to the way religion was perceived: a system of belief or thought imbedded in particular texts (for the most part Christian!). Religion as a cultural institution was taught in anthropology and sociology departments, if it was taught at all. Times, of course, have changed. Courses dealing centrally with religion as a cultural institution, including non-Western religions, now constitute an important component in religion department offerings, providing an excellent opportunity for the use of audio-visual instructional resources.

This essay speaks to this development. It will analyze Theravāda Buddhism within the cultures of Sri Lanka and Southeast Asia from the backgrounds of three differing social and political contexts: the traditional village, the kingdom and nation state, and the modern city and town. Each of these contexts provides a background for examining seminal themes in the study of religion and, more particularly, Buddhism in Southeast Asia; the integrative and syncretic nature of traditional, popular religion; the role of religion in political legitimation and national integration; and the response of traditional religion to the forces of modernization and rapid change. Good audio-visual resources are not equally available in each of these areas. Partially for this reason most of this essay will focus on traditional, institutional Theravāda Buddhism on the level of popular practice; however, the themes of political legitimation and modernization are of such significance that they could not be omitted.

This essay, then, provides an introduction to the study of Theravāda Buddhism and society within the cultural setting of Southeast Asia. In the broadest sense it is an examination of the interaction of "worldview" and "ethos," or the ways in which the peoples of Southeast Asia have organized and expressed their lives in meaningful patterns.[6] This essay analyzes these patterns in order to provide a coherence to their variety, and it correlates the analysis with an audio-visual instructional format. This guide, then, is both a self-contained study of Buddhism and Society in Southeast Asia as well as the basis of a semester's course or portion of a course into which audio-visual resources on this subject can be integrated.

CHAPTER 1

The Popular Tradition: Integration and Syncretism

ALL TOO OFTEN the Western understanding of Buddhism bears little resemblance to what the field researcher finds in Southeast Asia. The popular Theravāda traditions of Sri Lanka, Burma, Thailand, and Laos seem to be a badly distorted reflection of the cardinal teachings of *nibbāna*,[7] the Four Noble Truths, or the Eightfold Noble Path with which the Western student of Buddhism may be familiar. The observer enters a Theravāda Buddhist culture to discover that ordination into the monastic order (*saṅgha*) may be calculated for the meritorious benefit of one's mother rather than the pursuit of wisdom; that the noise of festival celebration drowns out the quiet atmosphere of meditation; that somewhat illkept village temples vastly outnumber forested hermitages; and that the Buddha, austerely imaged in his meditation posture or dispelling the forces of Māra testing his newly won enlightenment, is venerated in the hope of gaining privilege and prestige, material gain, and protection on journeys.

The seeming contradictions between the highest ideals and goals of Theravāda Buddhism and the lived tradition in Southeast Asia has been the subject of considerable Western consternation, confusion, and amazement, not to mention the stuff of numerous scholarly monographs. Decades ago Max Weber drew a distinction between the otherworldly goal of early Indian Buddhism and the more world-affirming nature of popular Buddhism under the reigns of monarchs like King Aśoka.[8] More recently Melford Spiro has contrasted nibbanic, or more ideal expressions of Burmese Buddhism with more popular and magical forms,[9] and Winston King's study of Theravāda ethics in that same country has been partially structured around the differentiation between the ultimate goal of *nibbāna* and more proximite, self-serving goals formulated in terms of the metaphysics of *kamma* and rebirth (*saṁsāra*).[10]

Any holistic account of Theravāda Buddhism in Southeast Asia must account for its highest ideals and practices as well as their seeming contraries as part and parcel of an integrated cultural-religious system. On a logical level the Theravāda belief in the no-soul (*anattā*) theory seems contradicted by merit-making ceremonies for the benefit of the soul of the deceased, just as the uninhibited consumption of rice whiskey by a proud father at the ordination of his son into the novitiate seems both inconsistent with the occasion and the ethical norm not to consume intoxi-

Buddhist Monastery Compound

cating beverages. Nevertheless, these contraries exist side by side and explanations that seek somewhat arbitrarily to differentiate teaching and practice, the ideal and the actual, run the risk of sacrificing the interwoven multiplicity of the fabric of religion to the logic of consistency.*

Keeping this admonition in mind we use the term *popular tradition* with some trepidation. No value judgment is intended. *Popular* does not mean less serious, less rigorous, or further from the ideal; rather, it is intended to mean Theravāda Buddhism as commonly perceived, understood, and expressed by the average, traditional Sri Lankan, Burman, Thai, and Laotian. What defines their sense of religious and cultural identity, the contexts in which this identity is most readily investigated, are rites of passage, festival celebrations, ritual occasions, and behavior as exemplified in traditional stories. We go to the temple or the temple-monastery to observe many of these activities and to hear the teachings as handed down orally from monk (*bhikkhu*) to layperson or to view their depiction in religious art. Institutionally the religious life of the Theravāda Buddhist focuses on this place of public worship, celebration, and discourse. Symbolically the temple-monastery is the "Buddha's place" (*Buddha-vassa*) as represented by his images and enshrined relics, its ceremonies, and often by its physical structure.

*Of the available films on Theravāda Buddhism in Southeast Asia *The Smile* most subtly raises the question of the seeming paradox between the ideal of Theravāda Buddhism correlated with goal of Nirvāṇa and the practice of meditation, and institutional Buddhism as it enters into the cultures of particular Southeast Asian countries.

This portion of the essay will examine popular Buddhism in Southeast Asia in the contexts mentioned above: rites of passage, festival celebration, ritual occasions, and ideal behavior or life models as embodied in traditional legends. The two underlying themes will be the syncretic nature of popular Buddhism as part of a total cultural system, and the function it serves to enhance life's meaning through personal, social, and cosmic integration and interpretation.

A. Ideal Action

Conceptually or discursively, ideal action in Theravāda Buddhism can be described as action that does not accrue merit or demerit, i.e., action beyond the power of *kamma* (skt., *karma*). Appropriate terms used to interpret ideal behavior and attitudes are "equanimity" (*upekkhā*), "compassion" (*karuna*), "righteousness," and "wisdom," to mention only a few. In both Theravāda and Mahāyāṇa Buddhism these virtues are referred to as perfections (*paramitā*) of character. In both traditions, one finds relatively elaborate discussions of them. Far from being abstractions, however, these virtues are embodied in the narratives of such heroes as Vessantara and Sama in the last ten of the 547 canonical *jātaka* tales[11] in the Theravāda scriptures, and, most importantly, in the life of the Buddha, himself. Such stories are well known and are the principal means through which ideal life models are taught.*

It may seem commonplace to emphasize the centrality of the Buddha for Theravāda Buddhism in Southeast Asia. Nevertheless, I do so with as much declarative power as possible for the simple reason that all too often course instruction may be devoted primarily to unpacking Buddhist doctrine or analyzing rituals and ceremonies to the near exclusion of that singular prince, Siddhattha Gotama, who was to become a universal figure, a Buddha or enlightened one.

Initially, of course, the Buddha must be understood as the founder of the tradition. Beyond that, however, his life-story becomes the paradigm for every devout follower who seeks the same enlightenment he achieved, especially the Buddhist monk. Prince Siddhattha responded to life perceived as old age, suffering, and death, by embarking on a quest which meant renouncing the life of the householder. He became a mendicant *bhikkhu* ("beggar"), studying and meditating until he discovered the true nature of human existence (i.e. *anicca, anattā*) which enabled hm to overcome suffering (*dukkha*) in its most profound ontological dimension. In an ideal sense every follower of the Buddha seeks the same enlightenment (*nibbāna*). *Nibbāna* is not merely an abstract concept; the Buddha embodies

*There are no generally satisfactory films on the life of the Buddha. *Gautama the Buddha* (1¼ hours), produced by the Government of India, uses statues, reliefs, paintings and architectural sites to help recreate the story of the Buddha. The narration and soundtrack on this film make it less than ideal for classroom instruction, however.

this mode-of-being-in-the-world, pointing to it as a reality to be achieved. While we cannot always ascertain the intentions which take a young Burman or Thai into the Buddhist *saṅgha* (monastic order), symbolically his ordination re-enacts the Buddha's story.*

The central teachings of Theravāda Buddhism emerge from the narrative of the Buddha's life. Broadly speaking the *sutta* literature of this tradition of Southeast Asian Buddhism represents episodes strung together as segments of the Buddha's life, much as pearls are strung on a single strand. Each pearl can be admired in and of itself but only when connected together by a thread do they make a necklace. Similarly, each *sutta* episode conveys particular teachings but these teachings are embedded in the larger framework of the Buddha's life. The Buddha's teaching (the *dhamma*) is inseparable from the young man who sought to see through the apparent contradictions and sufferings of life to a deeper truth, and having succeeded, taught this truth by word, deed and example.

When a Sri Lankan, Burman, Thai, or Laotian Buddhist enters a temple or approaches a pagoda (*cetiya*) he/she is, among other things, encountering the Buddha. The pagoda or *cetiya* reliquary enshrines his physical presence; images of varying poses (*mudras*) remind the viewer of the Buddha's struggle with the temptor Māra, his enlightenment, his teaching; and murals depict in a more representational manner long-remembered and embellished episodes from his life. Among the most frequent in occurrence are his miraculous birth; the four sights or scenes where he encounters old age, suffering, death, and a wandering truth-seeker; his enlightenment experience under the *bodhi* tree; and his first discourse to his five former disciples. The paintings tell a story, not just an inspired tale of the past but a present reality. The Buddha does not merely *symbolize* the overcoming of attachment, ignorance, and grasping, and the attainment of binary ideals of dispassion and compassion. He *is* that truth and that reality. He represents the occasion whereby those who follow his example may discover this truth for themselves, or, by relying on his power at least improve their lot in this life or a future one.

The Buddha's story, of course, does not stand alone as an ideal life model. In the Theravāda tradition the lives of saints, particularly in the form of *jātaka* tales purporting to be previous lives of the Buddha, embody particular virtues. They provide paradigms to be emulated rather than a discursive discussion of Buddhist doctrine. Of these, the most famous is the story of Prince Vessantara,[12] the last life of the Buddha prior to his incarnation as Siddhattha Gotama, and the embodiment of the perfection of generosity (*dāna*). The story begins with Vessantara, Prince of Sivi, giving up his kingdom's white elephant with magical rain-making powers to the neighboring kingdom of Kalinga to help overcome the drought they are experiencing. The citizenry of Sivi, incensed by this generous act, banish

*For a view of ordination as reenactment of the paradigmatic acts of the Buddha see *Buddhism: Be Ye Lamps Unto Yourselves.*

Vessantara and his family to the jungle. Before his departure he arranges a *dāna* or gift-giving ceremony where he gives away most of his possessions. Upon leaving the capital a group of Brahmins request his horse-drawn chariot which he willingly surrenders, afterwards proceeding on foot with his wife and two children into the forest. As we would expect and as the logic of true *dāna* requires, soon after Vessantara and his family are happily settled in their simple jungle hut, the prince is asked to give up his children to an old Brahmin, Jujāka. When Indra appears in disguise and Vessantara acceeds to the god's demand for his wife, the prince's trials come to an end. Having successfully met all of the tests of true generosity as arranged by the gods, Vessantara is restored to his family and succeeds his father as king of Sivi.

As the Buddha story embodies the ideals of *nibānna* and non-attachment, the Vessantara story illustrates the *kamma* doctrine, in this case a reward for the meritorious (*puñña*) action of generosity (*dāna*). Much has been made of the differences between nibbanic or noble-path action and kammic-merit motivated action. When they are placed within their well-known narrative contexts, however, the interrelationships become more readily apparent. Both Siddhattha and Vessantara exemplify modes of selflessness symbolized by a quest and a journey respectively in which renunciation marks the beginning of a critical liminal period preceding a return or restoration. In the Buddha's case the liminal state is one of intensive study and ascetical practice from which he emerges transformed as the Buddha. Vessantara's residence in the jungle represents his liminal stage from which he returns to be rewarded with a new dimension of secular power. Although the stories differ, they embody a similar structure. Furthermore, they focus on the virtue of selflessness: in Vessantara's case generosity (*dāna*), and in the Buddha's the total transformation of being symbolized by the term, *not-self* (*an-attā*), i.e., a state which cannot be designated by a "self" concept.

Many other tales serve to characterize different facets of both ideal and objectional behavior and their reward and/or punishment. Some of them illustrate the five precepts or training rules fundamental to the normative ethical system of popular Theravāda Buddhism in Southeast Asia: the prohibitions against taking life, stealing, lying, committing adultery, and drinking intoxicants. One such story relates the experience of the pious monk, Phra Malai, who was given the opportunity to visit the Buddhist hells, populated by those who had broken the precepts, and the heavens, enjoyed by those who had faithfully kept them, in order to instruct humankind about the kind of fate to expect. Temple murals also depict episodes from this popular story, not as a model of ideal behavior as in the case of the Buddha and Vessantara, but as a vivid way of reinforcing the basic Buddhist moral code.

Theravāda Buddhism teaches the ideals of selflessness, wisdom, and compassion which are identified with the person of the Buddha and the goal of *nibbāna*. It also establishes normative moral principles and rules necessary for social harmony. These rules are reinforced by such stories as the Phra Malai, and are elaborated by famous canonical *suttas* like the *Sigālovāda*, where the Buddha teaches a young Brahmin boy about the duties and responsibilities that should obtain among parent and child, husband and wife, teacher and student, friends, servants and masters, mendicants, and lay supporters. Southeast Asian Buddhism, of course, encompasses much more than the kinds of individual and social ideals represented by the Buddha, Vessantara, Phra Malai, and Sigala. In particular, it locates human beings within a complex cosmology of various divine, human, and demonic powers and provides a system for coping with them.*

B. Ritual Occasions, Merit, and the Appropriation of Power

Buddhist rituals can be classified in various ways. Melford Spiro, for example, characterizes Theravāda ritual action in Burma in terms of a fourfold typology: commemorative, expressive, instrumental, and expiatory.[13] Commemorative ritual is performed in remembrance of a historical, legendary, or mythological event; expressive ritual serves to manifest emotions and sentiments felt toward objects of reverence, e.g., Buddha, *dhamma*, *saṅgha*; instrumental ritual aims to achieve some goal in this life or in future lives; expiatory ritual is performed to atone for misdeeds.[14] Like most religious phenomena, rituals can be interpreted on several levels so that such a typology should not be taken as exhaustive nor should its separate categories be thought of as mutually exclusive. Furthermore, while rituals vary in nature, function and intent, an overarching perspective to be kept in mind is the one suggested above, namely, that Theravāda ritual in Southeast Asia provides a means for coping with a wide spectrum of powers.

As general descriptive categories these powers might be symbolized simply as Buddhist and nonBuddhist. Specific Buddhist symbols operative in this kind of ritual context are most often associated with the Buddha, himself, and include Buddha images, his relics enshrined in *cetiya* or reliquary mounds, the *saṅgha* or monastic order, and Buddha amulets. Those symbols associated with individual Buddhist monks thought to be particularly holy are an important extension of this set of symbols. Their power partakes of the power represented by the Buddha since they follow his *dhamma* or teaching, but, in another sense their powers parallel those of the Buddha. That is, their images, relics, and amulets may be venerated for their own sake, not essentially because of the holy man's relationship to the Buddha as founder of the tradition.

*The cosmology of reward and punishment is suggested in the discussions of merit-making in both *Buddhism: Footprint of the Buddha—India,* and *Buddhism: Be Ye Lamps Unto Yourselves.*

NonBuddhist symbols to which special powers are ascribed within ritual contexts which themselves may or may not be overtly Buddhist can be classified as animistic or Brahmanistic.[15] These would include Brahmanical deities such as Indra (the Theravāda Buddhist Sakka) and Viṣṇu, who might be invoked to guard the place and/or occasion of a Buddhist ceremony; the Hindu gods in Sri Lanka like Kataragama, i.e., Skanda, second son of Śiva, who exist in a hierarchical relationship to the Buddha;[16] and various indigenous deities and spirits such as the *nats* in Burma,[17] and the *cao* and *phī* in Thailand and Laos.[18] Some ritual occasions in Theravāda Southeast Asia may be primarily nonBuddhist, others specifically Buddhist, and still others various blends and combinations of Buddhist and nonBuddhist elements. As we shall see in the following discussion, most ritual occasions are syncretistic in one way or another. Broadly speaking, as a cultural institution a religion will inevitably be syncretistic. Furthermore, if religious ritual is seen as a system for coping with differing kinds of powers within a multiplex cosmology, we would expect particular ritual occasions to integrate symbols from different traditions in the service of this end. From this perspective, the particular historical identity of a symbol, i.e., Buddhist or nonBuddhist, is less significant than the total ritual context in which it functions.

In coping with power, Buddhist ritual in Southeast Asia functions in two primary ways: reciprocal exchange and appropriation. Reciprocal exchange emerges from a donor-donee situation typical of merit-making (*puñña*) rituals. The layperson-donor offers material gifts in support of the monastic order (*saṅgha*). In return the *saṅgha*-donee engenders a spiritual reward of merit (*puñña*), thereby enhancing one's balance of *kamma* which in turn effects the status of one's rebirth on the cosmic scale. Any ritual situation in which presentations are made to the monastic order function in this way. These would include acts as regular and informal as giving food to monks on their morning "alms" (*piṇḍapata*) rounds, to the annual and formal presentation of new robes and other gifts to the *saṅgha* at the end of the monsoon rains retreat (*vassa*) after the October full-moon day. The form of merit-making rituals in Theravāda Buddhism in Southeast Asia varies greatly; however, the structure of reciprocal exchange remains constant.

Other Southeast Asian religious rituals use somewhat different mechanisms for appropriating the power of the religious object. A pilgrimage to a famous *cetiya*-reliquary containing a Buddha relic; paying respects to a Buddha image with holy water lustrations during the New Year celebration in April; receiving and wearing an amulet containing the charred hair of a holy monk; "calling" spirits at times of crisis or life-junctures; making offerings to the deities of the four directions, the zenith and nadir: all of these ritual acts aim at appropriating power whether represented by the Buddha or other kinds of divine or demonic beings. Of course, elements of exchange can be found in these rituals as well. A gift is given, an offering made, a sum of money is paid in the expectation of some kind of return varying from an immediate and practical benefit to a general sense of well-being. Nevertheless, the structure of these rituals mirrors less clearly the reciprocal nature of merit-making exchanges. In the remainder of this analysis of Buddhist ritual in Southeast Asia we shall examine two different ceremonies that exemplify and justify this interpretation of ritual reciprocal exchange and appropriation of power. The first of these ceremonies is the presentation of new robes at the end of the monsoon rains retreat (*vassa*); the second is the consecration of a new Buddha image.*

Kathina Ceremony (Presentation of New Robes)

The presentation of new robes and other gifts at the end of the rains retreat takes its name from the robes offered at that occasion, namely, the *kaṭhina*. This ceremony takes place during the month immediately following the full moon sabbath (*uposatha*) day in October. According to the *Mahāvagga* of the Theravāda *Book of Discipline (Vinaya Piṭaka)* during a three month period from mid-July to mid-October monks were required to take up a settled residence and were allowed to leave this encampment only under special conditions. In this environment the mendicant nature of the Buddhist monkhood began to change. In particular, customs and practices of a collective life began to emerge including the recitation of a rule (*pāṭimokkha*) and the distribution of robes (*kaṭhina*). These ceremonies have continued through the ages and have evolved from culture to culture as the Theravāda form of Buddhism became normative in thirteenth century Sri Lanka and won the favor of ruling monarchs in Burma, Thailand, Laos, and Cambodia. Today in Thailand and Burma the *kaṭhina* ceremony provides one of the most popular occasions for merit-making. In village society this event usually involves the entire community, or in towns the monastery "parish" participates as a communal group.

The *kaṭhina* ceremony will last anywhere from one to sometimes three days. Although nearly every family in the community or parish will be involved in the preparation of foodstuffs and gifts offered to the monks at a particular monastery, the principal donor will probably come from another village, town, or region. This custom stems from the traditional view that greater merit accrues when the identity of the donor is unfamiliar to

*None of the films on Theravāda Buddhism do a particularly satisfactory job when it comes to presenting the more magical aspects of Buddhist ritual in Southeast Asia, probably because they focus on the normative dimensions of the Tradition. *The Temple of the Twenty Pagodas*, a somewhat impressionistic film about a Thai monastery-temple (*wat*) outside of Lampang, includes some provocative footage on amulets but fails to provide any explanation. *Buddhism: Footprint of the Buddha* includes a discussion of astrology in connection with an ordination ceremony.

†The reciprocal relationship between the monk and the laity is suggested in *Buddhism: Be Ye Lamps Unto Yourselves* and *Buddhism: Footprint of the Buddha* in their presentation of the monks alms rounds (*pindapata*). *Pindapata* is also covered in *Vejen*, a film focusing on the activities of a Burmese novice. Rains retreat ceremonies receive specific coverage in *Buddhism: Footprint of the Buddha* and *Chiang Mai, Northern Capital*. This latter film covers selected aspects of traditional northern Thai culture.

the *saṅgha.* In Thailand today this practice may also result from the fact that upcountry or rural monasteries are considered to be closer to the monastic ideal than rural ones. For this reason, affluent patrons from cities often sponsor *kaṭhinas* in the country. Most of the *kaṭhina* ceremonies I have witnessed followed this pattern. In one of the most memorable of these occasions, a set of robes completely spun and woven at the monastery within a twenty-four hour period was presented to the abbot of a rural northern Thai monastery famous for his austerity and prowess in meditation. Dozens of women were paid to card, spin, and weave in temporary quarters built for the occasion. In this case the sponsor was a wealthy business woman from Chiang Mai, the largest town in northern Thailand.

The actual presentation of robes, money and other offerings for the livelihood of the monks highlights the *kaṭhina.* It always involves a procession varying in size and constituency according to the nature of the community. Included will always be musical groups with instruments varying from traditional drums, cymbals and horns to school bands playing western musical instruments. Traditional dancers may be part of the processional entertainment and the marchers often wear traditional costume. In addition to the *kaṭhina* robes, symbolically the most important gift presented to the monastic order at this time, a "wishing tree" with money and other offerings[19] or a wooden palanquin representing a palace will occupy a place of honor in the procession. The palace-like conveyance represents the hope of the villagers that the merit they accrue in this celebration will enable them to live in a heavenly abode in some future lifetime.[20]

The procession winds its way through the streets of the town or village until it comes to the monastery proper. The participants file into the main assembly hall (*vihāra*) bearing robes, the wishing tree, and other palanquins filled with offerings of soap, towels, writing pads, canned food, cigarettes, and other material goods used by the monks. The ceremony itself begins as do most meetings of monks and laypersons with the lay leader of the congregation vowing the five basic precepts of Buddhist lay life: not to kill, lie, steal, engage in illicit sexual acts, or drink intoxicating beverages. Afterwards he leads the ritual of the presentation of gifts to the entire monastic community which are received on their behalf by the abbot. The chief donor then has the privilege of offering the first set of robes to the gathered monks but first presents them before a large Buddha image which dominates all such assembly rooms. The ceremony concludes when the monks and novices receive their new robes and chant an appropriate blessing.

A reciprocal transaction has taken place. In return for the offerings presented to the monastic order (*saṅgha*) the laity receive a spiritual blessing. In the calculus of merit-making (*puñña*) the participants hope for a reward in a future life brought about by the power of this good act.

But why is this particular ritual of exchange so important? All merit-making rituals are rooted in the symbolic role of the monastic order as mediator of the power represented by the Buddha, a power not only of supreme enlightenment but supernatural attainments. On this occasion the *saṅgha* has a special potency because for three months the monks have followed a somewhat more ascetic regime. In a sense the *kaṭhina* ceremony becomes the means by which the laity gains access to this potency and power. For this reason it is especially meritorious, and, furthermore, may be one of the explanations why possession of the *kaṭhina* robe, itself, confers on Burmese monks such privileges as being able to leave the monastery without the abbot's consent.[21] In short, the *kaṭhina* robe may be said to represent not only a particular period of tenure and training in the monastic order but also the spiritual power inherent in this position.

Image of the Buddha
Sukothai, Thailand—14th Century

Consecration of a Buddha Image

A second ceremony that helps us understand the fundamental significance of the transactional nature of Theravāda Buddhist ritual in Southeast Asia is the consecration of a Buddha image.[22] Nearly all Theravāda rituals that take place at the monastery occur in an assembly hall with a Buddha image. The image resides on a dias or altar making it higher in elevation than either the monks, who may sit on a raised platform, and the laity who sit on the floor. During most ceremonies which consist primarily of the chanting of Pāli texts and ritual chants composed in Pāli or vernacular languages, e.g. Burmese, Thai, Lao, a sacred thread attached to the Buddha image will be held by the monks, seemingly acting as a conduit of power residing in the image and magically released by the chant. In addition to being the visual focus of attention for any congregation performing a ritual act in the hall, the image also appears to be the object of such offerings as incense, candles, and flowers. When asked about the meaning of the offerings placed before a Buddha image most informants reply that they are given out of respect to the memory of the Buddha of which the image is a reminder, i.e., that the offerings are not given to the image itself. Such an interpretation coincides with the orthodox Theravāda view discouraging superhuman or magical interpretations of the Buddha. The ceremony in which a Buddha image is consecrated, however, would appear to contradict such a view.

In Theravāda Buddhist cultures the Buddha images installed in assembly halls (*vihāra*) must be formally consecrated. Until that takes place the statue is merely decorative, i.e., of no particular religious consequence. The consecration ceremony literally brings the image to life or empowers it, thereby transforming the image from its decorative and inconsequential status to one of spiritual and religious significance. After consecration an image becomes worthy of veneration, an object to which offerings are made not simply out of respect to the memory of a religious founder but with the expectation that an efficacious consequence will follow. Although one might argue on general psychological grounds that making an offering before a representation of a divine being or religious hero entails the hope of some sort of reward, acquaintance with an image consecration ceremony provides us with specific information regarding the fundamental dynamics of Theravāda Buddhist ritual.

An image consecration involves two primary elements, training the image and charging it with power. The ceremony proper which may be part of a larger celebration, lasts one night beginning at dusk and climaxing at dawn of the following day with the opening of the eyes of the Buddha image. Since the details of image consecrations differ among Theravāda cultures this description will be taken primarily from a ceremony I witnessed in northern Thailand in 1977. It was held at a small rural monastery outside of the town of Lamphun and was the occasion of several days of festivities which served the dual purposes of community celebration and raising money for the relatively impoverished monastery.

The ceremony was held in the assembly hall where the image was to be put in place. About dusk the monks and novices from the monastery and distinguished monks and ecclesiastical leaders from the district and province began chanting before a congregation of lay men and women who had packed the hall. The chanting began with selections from some of the *paritta* or "protection" *suttas* which became normative ritual texts in Sri Lanka and are widely used as the basis of most chanting services in

Southeast Asian Theravāda Buddhism. The entire evening was devoted to continuous chanting and sermons with the exception of about two hours between three and five a.m. During the night both monks and laity would wander in and out of the hall, an air of relaxed informality characterizing this otherwise serious affair. The collection of canonical and non-canonical texts chanted for this occasion rehearsed the life of the Buddha leading up to his enlightenment with a special emphasis on the supernatural attributes and powers acquired by him. The chanting concluded at dawn with the recitation of the First Discourse (*Dhammacakkapavattana Sutta*) performed while the eyes of the image were being uncovered.

During the entire night the image resided on the raised altar it would permanently occupy, its head covered with a white cloth and eyes sealed closed with honey symbolizing the unenlightened condition of the image, i.e., that it did not know its personal history, supernatural powers, or the *dhamma* ("truth"). The chanting of the monks and the sermons preached both instructed and empowered the image as the life history of the Buddha was traced. Prior to the ceremony various "gifts" for the image were placed before it including the five royal insignia (e.g., a fan), the eight requisites of a monk (e.g., a begging bowl), a small Bo tree, and a grass seat. These elements functioned as visual symbols of the story being told by the chanting monks of the prince who renounced the householder life, gained special powers through his training and ascetic practice, and finally attained to enlightenment. As the first rays of dawn reached out from the eastern horizon the white hood and honey were removed from the head and eyes of the image not only symbolizing the Buddha's enlightenment but indicating the completion of the training and empowerment of the image itself. Coincident with these acts three small mirrors which had faced the image were turned outward. These were said to represent the three types of superordinate knowledge achieved by the Buddha: knowledge of the future, of rebirth, and of *kamma*. Meanwhile, the monks and novices were chanting the First Discourse (*Dhammacakkapavattana Sutta*) the Buddha was reputed to have given after his enlightenment.

The image consecration ceremony dramatizes one of the fundamental polarities in Theravāda Buddhism, and also provides insight into the meaning of the mutual reciprocity that characterizes Theravāda merit-making rituals. The polarity is between virtuous wisdom and power. The Buddha embodies wisdom and virtuous perfections (*paramitā*), but also supernatural powers such as the divine eye and divine ear. On the one hand, the Theravāda chronicles of Sri Lanka, Burma, Thailand and Laos tell of numerous miraculous feats of the Buddha, among the most important being his magical flight to these countries thereby sanctifying the land. On the other hand, the Buddha cautions his followers against displays of supernatural power and defeats miracle workers with his *dhamma* or teaching. In Theravāda countries like Thailand, moreover, the qualities of the Buddha are often referred to by the couplet "power and virtue." The consecration of a Buddha image provides a particularly crucial focus for understanding the nature of the inter-relationship between these two qualities, especially in regard to the dynamics of Buddhist ritual.

What is the intentionality behind the offerings of incense, flowers, and candles before a Buddha image? While we do an injustice to the tradition to discount the normative rationale of paying respects to the memory of the teacher-founder, the desire to receive some sort of boon or benefit reflects the belief that the image itself has a special power to grant the wishes of the devotee. A similar dynamic lies behind merit-making rituals. By making an offering, especially a lavish and costly one, the donor hopes to effect a reciprocal response from the power infused into the Buddha image; hence, by knowing something about the nature of the image consecration ceremony we arrive at a more comprehensive understanding of rites like the *kaṭhina* robe presentation, and the integrated nature of the many facets of Theravāda Buddhist ritual.

On one level the *kaṭhina* ceremony can be interpreted as an appropriate annual renewal and replenishment of the clothing and other material requisites of the monastic order. Such an interpretation, however, ignores deeper levels of meaning which include the *saṅgha's* mediatorial role between the Buddha and the laity; the special sanctity of the monastic order following the more ascetical rains retreat period; and the extraordinary power of Buddha images in the reciprocal dynamic of merit-making rituals.

Omitted from our discussion so far has been the syncretic nature of Theravāda Buddhist ritual in Southeast Asia. Some rituals, like the presentation of *kaṭhina* robes may be relatively free of specific, insolatable nonBuddhist elements. Others like the image consecration ceremony traditionally include offerings to the guardians of the four quarters, the zenith and nadir, and A. K. Coomaraswamy has even argued that the ritual associated with opening the eyes of a Buddha image in Sri Lanka is fundamentally Hindu in character.[24] Other rites like those performed at such auspicious occasions as a change in professional status, twelfth cycle birthday celebrations, or even a trip abroad are fundamentally non-Buddhist in nature, even though Buddhist monks may play an important role in the ceremony.

In various ways the Buddhist rituals of Theravāda Buddhism can be seen to operate in terms of the metaphysics of action (*kamma*) and rebirth (*saṁsāra*), the power represented by the Buddha and his image, but also the power of all the gods and spirits beneficent and malevolent. The operational intentions of Theravāda rituals in Southeast Asia need to be understood from these varying and sometimes seemingly contradictory perspectives.

C. Festivals

The festival cycle of Theravāda Buddhism in Southeast Asia has two closely connected patterns, one agro-economic, the other Buddhist. The former reflects the rhythm of the agricultural year which moves from the rainy-planting season through the cool harvest season to the hot and dry fallow season. The second pattern is fashioned around a Buddhist calendar calculated in terms of seminal events in the tradition. Of particular significance are the birth, enlightenment, and death of the Buddha (*Visākhā Pūjā*); the occasion of the Buddha's First Discourse (*Āsāḷahā Pūjā*); and the gathering of 1250 *arahat* disciples at the Veluvana Mahāvihāra monastery where the Buddha preached on the *paṭimokkha*, i.e. the 227 rules of the discipline (*Māgha Pūjā*). These three celebrations appear to be roughly isomorphic with the triple gem of Theravāda Buddhism, i.e. the Buddha, the Dhamma, and the Saṅgha. Other important occasions in the religious year include the beginning and end of the rains retreat period (*vassa*), and the lifetime of the Buddha prior to his rebirth as Siddhatta Gotama when, as Prince Vessantara, he was the perfect exemplification of the moral perfection of charity (*dāna-paramitā*).

As scholars have observed, the religious festival calendar has a striking articulation with the phases of the agro-economic year.[24] We might note, for example, that *Visākhā Pūjā* occurs in May at the beginning of the Southeast Asian rice planting season; *Āsāḷahā Pūjā* in July during the growing season; and *Māgha Pūjā* during the period of harvest in February. Of course, the intertwining of the definitive events within a religious tradition with an annual life cycle pattern of a community should not surprise us since a similar integration can be found in both Christianity and Judaism. For example, Christmas anticipates the dawn of a new year with longer and brighter days, and Easter celebrates the renewal of Spring.

Visākhā Pūjā

Within the yearly rhythm of Theravāda Buddhism as a historical tradition *Visākhā Pūjā* stands as the most sacred of all anniversary occasions for the obvious reason that it celebrates the life of the Buddha. From the perspective of the tradition, the day itself is miraculous for on the full moon day of the month of Visākhā the Buddha was born, attained enlightenment, and died. In short, *Visākhā Pūjā* celebrates the entire story of the Buddha from its beginning to its climax and on to its final conclusion. Although in countries like Thailand this triple anniversary was once celebrated over three days, at the present time only one day has been set aside as a national holiday. The manner of its observance varies among different Theravāda cultures. In Sri Lanka night processions with Vesak (i.e. *Visākhā*) lanterns mark the occasion.* In Thailand and Burma evening activities predominate. Instead of festive processions, however, crowds gather in the monastery compounds to circumambulate three

*The preparation for and celebration of *vesak* in Sri Lanka forms the substance of a film by the same name directed by Yvonne Hanneman. The focus is on the popular celebration, particularly the elaborate Vesak lanterns, a theme picked up in the film, *Meditation*, where the accidental burning of a boy's Vesak lantern is used to symbolize Buddhism's teaching about the transcience of life.

times around the sacred precincts holding candles and burning incense, and to place elaborate decorations of flowers shaped like lotus buds before the Buddha altar. The faithful then enter the assembly hall to hear a discourse on the life of the Buddha which in less urbanized parts of Thailand may last most of the night.

One of the scriptures traditionally preached on this night is the *Pathamasambodhi* written in twenty-nine chapters or sections. This text fills in the details of the Buddha's life story which are structured around the three events Viskāhā Pūjā incorporates. Since the sights and sounds of the festival itself may divert us from the doctrinal significance of this event we enter the assembly hall for an all-night reading of the text which we summarize under the following headings:

> (1) the wedding of Suddhodana and Mahāmāyā, the Buddha's parents; (2) the Buddha in Tusita heaven, beseeched by the gods to help mankind, enters the womb of Mahāmāyā; (3) the birth of the Buddha and the miraculous appearance on the same day of his future wife, Yasodhara, his beloved disciple, Ānanda, his horse, Channa, and his charioteer, Kanthaka, and the Bo tree; (4) two predictions by Brahmans, one that he will be either a world ruler or a Buddha, and the other that he is destined to become a fully enlightened one because he possesses the thirty-two marks of the great man (*mahāpurusa*); (5) the Buddha is given the name, Siddhattha; his mother dies after seven days; Siddhattha marries Yasodhara at age sixteen; (6) the four encounters — aged person, sick person, corpse, mendicant — prompt the Buddha to follow the mendicant path; (7) Siddhattha follows an ascetic way, e.g., abstaining from food, restraining his breath, for six years, then adopts a middle path as more appropriate to mind development; his five followers desert him; (8) Sujātā makes a food offering to the Buddha thinking he is a tree spirit; the Buddha's begging bowl miraculously moves upstream as a sign he will become enlightened; the Buddha determines not to move from his seat under the Bo tree until he realizes his highest goal; (9) Māra and his forces attack the Buddha; he successfully wards them off by calling the Goddess of Earth (Nāng Thorani) to witness on his behalf; the Goddess of Earth drowns the forces of Māra by wringing out the water from her hair that she had collected every time the Buddha performed an act of virtuous generosity (*dāna*); (10) attainments immediately prior to enlightenment — the eight trance states, knowledge of the previous conditions of all men, clairvoyance, the cycle of Dependent Coorigination (*paṭicca samuppāda*); the Buddha's enlightenment; (11) the Buddha spends seven days each at seven places after his enlightenment, e.g., the Bo tree, the location where he surveys the Abhidhamma, the place where Mucalinda, the serpent king, protects him from the rain, the spot where Indra and his first two lay followers make offerings; (12) the Buddha worries whether the people will be able to understand his teaching; the gods of Brahmalōka perceive his concern and send messengers to assure him that among humankind are persons who will be able to comprehend his message; (13) the Buddha teaches the

First Discourse (*Dhammacakkappavattana Sutta*); (14) the five former followers of the Buddha to whom his first teaching was given become saints (*arahats*); more people become disciples; (15) the Buddha's activities in Uruvela; the Buddha impresses King Bimbasara of Rājāgṛha; (16) Sāriputra and Moggalāna become followers of the Buddha; (17) Suddhodana requests the Buddha to come to Kapilavastu; his people become the Buddha's disciples; (18) Yasodhara's sorrow over her husband's rejection of the princely role; (19) Devadatta, the Buddha's cousin, attempts to kill the Buddha and then to split the Sangha; he is punished by the earth swallowing him up; (20) the Buddha predicts the future coming of the Buddha Meitreya and tells Ānanda that the monk with the lowest seniority will be the next reborn as Meitreya; (21) the Buddha heals his father's illness and he becomes an *arahat* before his death; an order of nuns is established on Ānanda's request but not equal to that of the *bhikkhusaṅgha*; (22) the Buddha performs several miracles but forbids his disciples to do so without seeking permission; (23) the Buddha travels to Tāvatimsa heaven and preaches the *Abhidhamma* to his mother; (24) the Buddha descends from Tāvatimsa heaven on a crystal ladder given by Indra; the Buddha goes to the top of Mount Sumeru where he performs a miracle witnessed by all from the hells (*Pretaloka*) to the heavens (*Brahmaloka*); (25) the death of Sāriputra and Moggallāna; (26) the Buddha's death (*parinibbāna*); (27) the Buddha's funeral; collecting the Buddha relics; the rulers of the major petty kingdoms of northern India come to request relics; (28) Mahākassapa buries the remainder of the relics which are not unearthed until the time of Asoka who divides them among various cities in India; (29) reasons for the decline of Buddhism in India.[25]

In northern Thailand the celebration of *Visākhā* may coincide with the annual anniversary of the founding of a major temple. When this occurs the length and extent of the festivities will be significantly increased. I witnessed one such occasion which included traditional northern Thai long drum and hot air balloon competitions as well as numerous temple processions and a symbolic cleansing of the monastery's Buddha relics.[26] Although for many participants the meanings of these events have been lost, others, especially those who were novices or monks in their youth, are capable of interpreting them from the pre-modern traditions of northern Thai Buddhism. Such festivals become a blending of the normative events of Theravāda Buddhism, i.e., the birth, enlightenment, and death of the Buddha, and more culturally relative customs. They celebrate both a particular Buddhist community within a given cultural and social context, and that community's identity as part of a universal tradition stretching back over 2500 years.

Our study of *Visākhā Pūjā* and the *kaṭhina* ceremony complement one another. The transactional nature of the *kaṭhina* as a merit-making ritual depends for its meaning on an understanding of the Buddha as a person of special power, a power embodied by the image itself. *Visākhā* demonstrates the significance of the Buddha's life story as a historical paradigm from which the Buddhist tradition takes its definition. The Buddha story is a constant referent for the tradition. Neither the Buddha's teaching (*dhamma*) nor his power can be abstracted from his person; and, for Theravāda Buddhism, his person is unfolded in the episodic history of a text like the *Pathamasambodhi* rather than a metaphysical claim about the Buddha's absolute and universal nature.

Loi Krathong

Religious festivals serve many functions, some more central than others to the normative religious tradition within a given culture. Whereas *Visākhā* provides an example of a celebration close to the core of Theravāda Buddhism in Southeast Asia, the Festival of Lights or the Festival of the Floating Boats (Thai: *loi krathong*) has little to do with Buddhism and might be characterized as animistic or Brahmanical in nature. It has, nevertheless, become at least partially assimilated into the Theravāda Buddhist cultural traditions of countries like Burma, Thailand, and Laos. This festival can serve as an example of religious syncretism in which the major import of the event does not have a Buddhist meaning.*

Loi Krathong is celebrated on the full moon day of November, one month after the end of the monastic rains retreat (*vassa*). Traditionally, in many parts of Thailand it coincided with a specifically Buddhist ceremony, the preaching of the long story of Prince Vessantara, the Buddha's last existence before his rebirth as Siddhattha Gotama. At this time the rainy season has come to an end, the rice crops have been planted, and the weather is turning pleasantly cool in the evenings. The farmers have a month or more before the rice crops need to be harvested. In this off-work season with flooded fields and moderate climate, people traditionally take time to enjoy themselves in the Festival of the Floating Boats. The celebration is a very simple one with no apparent connection to either Buddhistic or Brahmanical ritual. Small boats are made either from natural substances like banana stalks or leaves or, in recent years, from commercial products, and floated on rivers or ponds. On the boats will be placed lighted candles, incense and coins of small denominations. Everyone participates, elders watching the bobbing lights on the water and the children often swimming out to retrieve the most beautiful *krathongs* ("leaf cup") or the coins that might be found on them. Couples picnic nearby and youngsters may enjoy themselves with locally made fireworks. In northern Thailand houses may be decorated and in the provincial capital city of Chiang Mai, the *Loi Krathong* festival has taken on the overtones of a commercial success with parade of large floats through the city.

*The *loi krathong* celebration in northern Thailand is justly famous. Even though it is becoming overly commercialized in Chiang Mai, the northern capital, the quiet beauty of the lighted *krathongs* on the northern rivers and the community spirit experienced in the celebration make it particularly delightful to observe and participate in. *Chiang Mai, Northern Capital* has a good sequence on *loi krathong*. *Thailand, The Land of Smiles*, generally a much less satisfactory film, ends with a short segment on *loi krathong*.

The historical roots and meaning of *Loi Krathong* are ambiguous. It may have some connection with the Indian festival of lights, *Dīpavali*, or with a traditional Chinese custom of floating lotus flower lamps to guide the spirits of people drowned in rivers and lakes. The earliest evidence of the celebration in Thailand comes from the Sukhothai period when the second queen of King Phra Ru'ang (c.A.D. 1300), the daughter of a Brahmin family attached to the Court, began the custom in order to please the king. Such an explanation would appear to indicate an Indian Brahmanical origin for *Loi Krathong*. Two Buddhist explanations of a mythological nature have been advanced: that the *krathongs* carry offerings to a footprint of the Buddha put on the sandy shore of the Nammada River in the Deccan by the King of the Nāgā (serpents) who wanted to worship the Lord after his death;[27] that the river festival is an expression of gratitude to the King of the Nāgā, Phra Upagota, when he foiled Māra's attempt to destroy 84,000 *cetiyas* ("reliquaries") built by King Aśoka.[28] Although these two etiologies differ, they both point in the direction of the popular devotionalism which characterizes much of lay Theravāda Buddhist practice in Southeast Asia.

In northern Thailand a historical explanation for the origin of *Loi Krathong* prevails. During the reign of King Kamala of Haripuñjaya in the tenth century A.D. (modern day Lamphun, thirty kilometers to the south of Chiang Mai) a cholera epidemic of such severity broke out that the populace of the city was forced to evacuate. Eventually they found their way to Pegu (today located in Burma), where they stayed for six years until the epidemic subsided. After the majority of the people returned to Haripuñjaya they sent gifts of food and clothing down the river to their relatives who remained in Pegu.[29] The festival of *Loi Krathong* celebrates this event, or we might say that it becomes an annual offering to the spirits of the departed ancestors. Another explanation is that the *krathongs* are offerings to the Goddess of the *Mae Khongkha* (i.e., Ganges), the Mother of Waters.[30] Whatever the historical roots or the explanation of the festival of *Loi Krathong*, however, it remains one of the most picturesque celebrations in Thailand. To be sure, its connections with normative Theravāda Buddhism in Southeast Asia are tenuous. Buddhist rationalizations have been provided for it, and where Buddhist temples are found near rivers where the leaf boats are floated, people will take them into the temple compound to be blessed or to circumambulate the sacred precincts before putting the *krathong* in the water; however, *Loi Krathong* remains one of those festivals which has retained its basic nonBuddhist character. Perhaps for this reason both traditionally and at the present time Buddhist monasteries in some places in Thailand pick this night for the preaching of the Vessantara Jātaka story, thereby exploiting a celebratory occasion for their own purposes.

D. Rites of Passage

Buddhism in Southeast Asia has not only integrated into its own sacred history a community's annual agro-economic rhythm, but has marked and celebrated important junctures in the life cycle of the individual as well. In doing so Theravāda Buddhism has syncretized in varying degrees other religious modalities, in particular, an indigenous animism aimed at propitiating unseen and powerful spirits. Birth rites and weddings have traditionally had little or no connection with Theravāda Buddhism but puberty initiatory rites, which have taken the form of entrance into the monastic order for varying lengths of time, and funeral celebrations have been fundamental expressions of the integration of Southeast Asian Buddhism into the life cycle of the individual. Of these two rites of passage, the ordination ceremony often has a distinctly animistic part as prelude to ordination into the Buddhist novitiate or monkhood, while the funeral has nonBuddhist elements integrated into a structure and interpretative framework basically consonant with a Theravāda Buddhist cosmology. These rites have meanings on various levels: to insure safe passage through a transition to another stage of life; to integrate the life cycle of the individual into the ongoing life-pattern of the community; to place the individual within a cosmological structure governed by various unseen and relatively unpredictable powers (e.g., *kamma, cao, phī, nat*). The remainder of this section will study the Theravāda Buddhist ordination and funeral ceremonies, not only because they have film documentation, but because "In no other rites of passage . . . is Buddhism so directly concerned with a human event."[31]

*Ordination**

Ordination into the Theravāda Buddhist monkhood can be interpreted on a variety of levels. Normatively the monk is a "religious virtuoso"; that is, in seeking ordination he commits himself to a lifetime pursuit of the highest goal in Buddhism, Nibbāna, within the context of the monastic order (*bhikkhu saṅgha*). The Pāli term *bhikkhu* means one who has given up ordinary pursuits of livelihood for a higher goal, and becomes a mendicant or "beggar." The monk's begging "... is not just a means of subsistence, but an outward token that he has renounced the world and all its goods and has thrown himself for bare living on the chances of public charity."[32] The *Dhammapāda*, probably the most famous of all the Theravāda texts, characterizes the doctrinal ideal of the monk (*bhikkhu*) as follows: The true monk is one whose senses are restrained and who is controlled in body and speech. He is contented with what he receives; is not envious of others; and has no thought of himself. Such selflessness is rooted in the Buddha's truth (*dhamma*), and the monk who dwells in and meditates on the *dhamma* is firmly established in the Truth (*saddhamma*). Such a being is suffused with loving kindness (*mettā*), possesses the cardinal virtues, is refined in conduct, and is filled with a transcendental joy. Confident in the Buddha's teachings, having attained peace and supreme bliss, the monk "illumines this world like the moon from a cloud."[33] In short, the ideal monk is one

*See *Buddhism: Be Ye Lamps Unto Yourselves* which is built around two ordination ceremonies.

Two newly ordained monks, Lamphun, Thailand

who seeks and attains the truth. Having reached this goal he becomes a transformed moral being, irradiating the Buddha's *dhamma* for the benefit of humankind.

While some enter the monastery in order to seek Nibbāna, others fall short of this ideal. Melford Spiro analyzed Burmese men's motives for entering the monkhood into three conscious types — religious motives, the desire to escape the difficulties and miseries of human life, the wish to obtain an easier living[34] — and three unconscious motives — dependency, narcissism, and emotional timidity.[35] (Needless to say, Spiro's study of the motivational structure of monastic recruitment in Burma was not received with wild enthusiasm in that country!) Other somewhat more socially descriptive reasons for entering the monastery include acquisition of an education, achieving a higher social status, response to social custom and pressure, and repayment of a filial debt, especially to one's mother. Before analyzing the ordination ceremony itself, we shall briefly examine some of these motives.

In Burma, Thailand, and Laos, monastic tenure varies greatly in length depending upon the motivation for ordination. In short, unlike the West, becoming a monk does not involve a lifetime commitment. In Thailand one of the principal reasons for being ordained is to acquire an education. Among poorer families children often cannot be supported to attend school. Ordination as a novice takes care of their material needs, and also provides them with a basic education. Indeed, in Thailand if a boy is bright and highly motivated he may complete secondary school as a novice, graduate from a monastic college and earn an advanced degree from an Indian university. After a nominal period of one or two years teaching in a monastery school or serving as an administrator in a larger provincial monastery he will then probably disrobe and take a responsible and respected job in the secular world. Although such exploitation of the monastic educational structure siphons off able leadership, it has become standard practice and bears little social stigma.

Undoubtedly this pattern of being educated in monastic schools and then leaving the Order reflects an earlier practice where a young man would be ordained as a novice at about the age of puberty; remain in the monastery for a period of two to four years; and then return to lay society. During that period he would have received a basic education in the "Three Rs," would have learned the fundamentals of Buddhism, and would have been prepared to lead a responsible life as a lay Buddhist supporter of the monastic order. This particular pattern, still followed in some local areas of Southeast Asia, makes ordination into the monkhood closer to a rite of passage into adulthood. In this sense, its Western parallel would be the rite of confirmation in the Christian tradition or Bar Mitzvah in the Jewish. Traditionally these ceremonies symbolized full participation in their respective communities, just as having been ordained a Buddhist monk would have been an essential stage in the passage to mature adulthood in Thai, Lao, or Burmese society and culture.

Although one takes a vow of celibacy and is forbidden to acquire material goods, being a monk does not involve ascetic practice. Theravāda Buddhism in Southeast Asia consistently upholds the time-honored tradition of the "Middle Way." In practice, the monk lives a reasonably comfortable life and occupies a respected status in the community. For children of poorer families, in particular, becoming a monk represents a definite improvement in their social status. For this reason it is not surprising to find that the majority of Burmese and Thai monks do, in fact, come from relatively impoverished backgrounds. For instance, at the two monastic colleges in Bangkok, over ninety percent of the students come from the northeastern section of the country which happens to be the most economically disadvantaged area of the country.

Finally, it should be noted that being ordained is perceived as a way of repaying a debt to one's parents, especially one's mother. That one has come into the world, survived infancy and become a youth results primarily from the care of one's mother. Within the calculus of meritorious action (*puñña*), to be ordained gains a spiritual benefit for one's parents. The mutual reciprocity characterizing merit-making ritual becomes part of ordination into the monastic order. A young man survives infancy due to the material benefits provided by his mother and father; he returns to them a spiritual boon by being ordained.

A village ordination in northern Thailand will typically be held on one or two days, and will be divided into two parts. The first is an animistic ceremony called "making the spirits" or "calling the spirits"; the second is the ordination into the novitiate or, if the candidate is twenty or older, higher ordination. The first part of the ceremony will probably be held in the ordinand's home, and will be the occasion of village-wide festivities with as much feasting, drinking, and general merry-making as the young man's family can afford. The spirit-calling ceremony will be conducted by a layman who performs such roles at weddings, house dedications and other auspicious or crisis occasions. He would have been ordained a monk for several years earlier in his career when he would have learned the texts involved in these rituals as well as the methods of chanting and preaching. His ritual role differs from that of the monk but rivals it in importance.[36]

During the ceremony the lay leader entices or calls the ordinand's thirty-two spirits (Thai: *khwan*) from any previous attachment to their enjoyment of lay life so that the youth will make the transition to the celibate life of the monk undivided and completely integrated in purpose and intention. To insure that the young man's spirits are properly enticed, a special offering bowl is prepared for them with bananas, eggs, water, and cigarettes or fermented tea leaves. A sacred thread is then tied around the wrists of the ordinand symbolizing the tying of the *khwan* into his body.

Before the spirit-calling ritual the ordinand will have been properly prepared for his ordination. His head and facial hair is shaved and he is clothed in a white robe. Both acts symbolize a transition state between the stage of the householder and the monk, a necessary neutering of one's previous self-definition before taking on the monastic vocation with a new name. It also symbolizes the monk's disregard for the things of this world, including the vanities of personal appearance. Upon the conclusion of this nonBuddhist ritual the ordinand, his family, friends and well-wishers form a procession to the monastery compound. Often the young man will be dressed as Prince Siddhattha and will ride on a horse to the ordination hall reenacting the "great renunciation" of the Lord Buddha. The procession circles around the ordination hall (*uposatha*) three times. Before entering it the ordinand bows before the boundary stone (*sīma*) at the front entrance invoking the Buddha to forgive his sins and to grant him blessings. The sacrality of the ordination hall and, hence, the significance of the ordination ceremony (*upasampadā*) is indicated by the nine *sīma* stones marking its center and the eight directional points around its perimeter. Traditionally women were not allowed to enter the ordination hall, a practice which has been largely discontinued in Thailand.

Entering the hall, one of his friends may act the role of Māra pretending to prevent his entrance, or he may fling a last handful of coins to the well-wishers who have followed him. He approaches the chapter of ten monks seated on the floor in a semicircle in front of a large Buddha image resting on a raised altar at the far end. Bowing to the floor three times before the monastery's abbot who will conduct the ordination ceremony, he presents him with gifts of candles, incense, and robes. Professing the Buddha, his teaching (*dhamma*) and the monastic order (*saṅgha*) to be his refuge, he requests permission three times to enter "the priesthood in the Vinaya Dhamma of the Blessed One."[37] The abbot receives the robes, instructs the ordinand in the Three Gems (i.e. Buddha, *dhamma, saṅgha*) and the five bodily meditations before another monk designated as the young man's instructor (*ācariya*) formally introduces him to the Ten Precepts upheld by all monastic novices: to refrain from taking life, stealing, sexual intercourse, lying, intoxicating beverages, eating at forbidden times, entertainments, bodily adornments, sleeping on comfortable beds, and receiving money. Having taken the precepts, once again the ordinand approaches the abbot. This time he is assigned to a senior monk as an instructor and given a Pāli name. The instructor hangs his begging bowl over his left shoulder and has the young man identify his bowl and three monastic robes before taking him aside to question him on behalf of the entire chapter. His formal queries include, "Do you have leprosy?" "Are you a human?" "Are you free of debt?" "Do you have permission from your parents?" Being found free of impediments, the instructor then presents the ordinand to the chapter requesting that they admit him into the monastic order. Agreeing to the request by their silence, the assembled chapter receives the young man as a novice. The ceremony concludes with the abbot giving him instruction in the life of a monk.

The ordination ceremony provides an extraordinary opportunity to understand the richness of Theravāda Buddhism as a cultural institution in its Southeast Asian context. Normatively it represents the highest ideals of the doctrinal tradition; symbolically it offers a reenactment of the most dramatic event of the Buddha's life narrative; structurally it illustrates the fundamental movement of a rite of passage; sociologically it provides evidence for the syncretic nature of Southeast Asian Buddhism even in one of its most essential expressions. For these reasons the use of film and other audio-visual material as part of a study of the ordination ceremony should be put to particularly effective use.

Monks chanting before a coffin

*Funeral Rites**

Entrance into the monastic order represents a passage into an altered mode of existence, ideally one dedicated to the pursuit of a goal which will free the monk from the power of determinative actions (*kamma*) and rebirth (*saṁsāra*), and the generally unsatisfactory condition (*dukkha*) of merely mundane (*lokiya*) existence. Death marks another passage, one fraught with ambiguity for the deceased as well as for the living. Consequently, it is acknowledged by rites which assure the survivors of their own well-being as well as the benefit of the departed. To modern Western eyes a traditional funeral rite in Burma or Thailand may appear unusually festive. One must keep in mind, however, that the funeral not only honors the deceased and mourns his/her loss, but also affirms the continued existence of the family and the community. Funerals, then, not only acknowledge the fact of death, but celebrate life.

*Despite the significance of funerary rites in Southeast Asian Buddhism only *Buddhism: Be Ye Lamps Unto Yourselves* has a funeral sequence. Funerary rite slides are also included in *Buddhism in Southeast Asia and Ceylon*.

Funerary rites in Theravāda Buddhist Southeast Asia may be held in the home or at the temple, and will vary in many details depending on the type of death – e.g., from old age or accident, the wealth of the deceased, whether a monk or lay person – and the local customs of a particular area. The main ritual officiants will be Buddhist monks; the ritual chants will be from such normative Buddhist texts as the *Abhidhamma* ("higher teaching"); and the traditional funeral sermon will deal with the themes of punishment and reward, the impermanence of life (*anicca*), and the ultimate goal (*nibbāna*) beyond the polarity of life and death. The rites themselves, however, incorporate many nonBuddhist elements designed to ward off the threatening powers of evil associated with death, and are even more thoroughly syncretic than the ordination ceremony.

Several good descriptions of Buddhist funerals in Southeast Asia are available.[38] The following explanation will be based on my own observations of funerals in central and northern Thailand as well as several ethnographies.[39] Near the moment of death Buddhist *mantras* may be whispered into the ear of the dying, in all probability the four syllables symbolizing the structure of the *Abhidhamma* – *ci, ce, rū,* and *ni* (mind, mental concepts, body, and *nibbāna*) – or written on a piece of paper and put in his/her mouth.[40] At death there may be an extended period of loud wailing, in part to announce to a village community that a death has occurred. After removing the deceased's clothes the body will be washed, sometimes interpreted as a cleansing for the passage of the soul to heaven. The hands will be clasped together over the chest and a thread will be passed three times around the hands, toes, and neck symbolizing the bonds of passion, anger, and ignorance. Before cremation these will be removed representing the release from these bonds (*nivāraṇa*) by the power of charity, kindheartedness, and meditation.[41]

Several items will be placed at the head of the corpse. They may include food for the person's spirit to eat and water for it to drink, a kerosene lamp to light its way to the other world, and a three-tailed white flag representing the Three Gems. Flowers and incense will be put in the deceased's hands, traditional offerings before Buddha images representing the Buddha's teachings and concentration of the mind. Finally, a coin may be put in the corpse's mouth or a small set of silver and golden flags will be placed by the body to abet the soul's entrance to heaven.

After the body is put in a coffin the cremation may take place immediately or be deferred a week or even longer. In the case of distinguished monks the period between death and cremation may be extended up to a year. The coffin, itself, will be made from plain wood planks, the three forming the bottom being said to represent the three levels of the Buddhist cosmology: the realm of desire, form, and the formless realm. When the coffin is taken from the house, the feet will be pointed to the west, the direction of death, symbolizing the reversal of life by death. The wooden house steps may be replaced by a temporary set of stairs with only three steps, representing the tripartite cosmological structure of Theravāda

Buddhism.[42] When the temporary stairs are taken down and the coffin burned, it is hoped that the deceased has been freed from these conditions and has reached Nibbāna.

The days between the actual death and the funeral and cremation are ones of busy activity. If a normal death of a moderately well-off villager, the family of the deceased will be joined by relatives and friends preparing for evening festivities. Local orchestras will entertain guests, and there will be extraordinary feasting, drinking, and gambling. During the day monks will be invited to the home for funeral chants, and gifts will be presented to them in order to earn merit for the deceased. Although the noisy evening activities may be interpreted as a means of encouragement against the dead person's ghost, their primary function appears to be a reenforcement of community solidarity and integration in the face of the threat of death.

On the day of the funeral, selected for its auspicious signs for the deceased, the coffin is taken in procession from the home to the temple or to the cremation grounds. The size and extent of the procession varies according to the wealth and status of the deceased. I once witnessed a funeral procession in Chiang Mai, northern Thailand, of a distinguished abbot whose coffin was borne on an elaborate funeral car in the form of a mythological elephant-bird in which thousands of people wound their way through the streets of the city. For this event distinguished monks from all over the country were invited and one hundred young men were ordained as novices to make merit for the deceased.

Before the cremation a final preaching service will be held. The monks will chant, and a sermon will be delivered. A typical rural northern Thai sermon might include some of the following remarks:[43]

> Dear friends, I was invited to deliver a speech to you who are attending this merit-making for the dead Mr. Khiow. A good Buddhist presents his guests with two things, good food and accommodations, and a sermon by a priest to take back home with them. Today I will preach to you about death.
>
> Death is a common event that will come to everyone without exception. Nobody can live forever, but everybody must die sooner or later. Some people say that a dead person is only trouble to his relatives and friends who stay behind. Dead animals are more useful to us than dead people because we can use their hide, bones, and meat. The only things left by a dead person are his good deeds, which we can remember.
>
> We go to the funeral of a dead person just as if we were going to see off a good friend when he is leaving for another country. Now we have come to see Mr. Khiow off to another world. We do not like to see him go, but when his time came he had to leave. Nobody could stop him, all we are able to do is to make merit and transfer merit to him. . . .
>
> Everybody must remember that we all have to die, not only the person whose funeral we are attending today. Before death comes, we must prepare ourselves for it. The Lord Buddha did not cry

> when death was approaching because he knew the meaning of death. We cry when we see death because we do not have the knowledge of a Buddha.
>
> The Lord Buddha said, "Death is the change of the name and the body of a spirit from one form to another." Nothing in the world, even life or matter, can vanish; it only changes.
>
> To the question where the spirit of a dead person goes, we can say that it is reborn. In Buddhism we say that a person with an unclean spirit of covetousness, anger, and ill temper will be reborn again, but he who has a clean spirit will go straight to Nibbāna. The Lord Buddha had a clean spirit; so after his death, his spirit went straight to Nibbāna without being reborn again. . . .
>
> I cannot speak any longer because I have already taken a long time. Before ending, I shall suggest again that death is not a strange event; it does not belong to any particular person, but to all of us. We will die when our time comes, the time being scheduled by Phaja-Madcura-d, who is the chief of death.
>
> If I should receive any merit for this preaching, I beg to dedicate it to Mr. Khiow. I ask that this merit may help and support him in the right place, or give him a chance to be reborn in a good place. If his spirit should still be wandering around some place, because of his attachment to his family or his property, I beg that this merit lead him from these earthly attachments to some other place.
>
> Finally, I beg for the blessings of the Lord Buddha to come upon you and bring you long life, a light complexion, happiness, and good health.

The cremation itself may take several forms: the wooden coffin may be burned on a pyre of wood; the coffin and funeral car may be burned through an elaborate process of igniting rockets and firecrackers; or, as in Bangkok, it may be burned in a crematory oven. Prior to the cremation, the monks attending the funeral approach the coffin and remove sets of robes placed on it to earn special merit for the deceased. While picking up the robes the monks chant the following Pāli stanza:

> All the aggregates which causation has brought together are not permanent; they arise and disappear; they arise and are extinguished; they are not permanent and abiding. When the aggregates become quieted or stopped, peace ensues, and that which causes suffering no longer afflicts us.

Numerous elements comprise the funeral rite in Southeast Asian cultures. Although the ceremony is conducted by Buddhist monks, much that takes place and the interpretations given vary considerably from normative Theravāda Buddhism. In particular, the spirit or soul (*viññāna*) of the deceased is perceived as a powerful agent which must be treated properly in a ritual sense to ensure its future wellbeing and to avoid retribution on the surviving family and friends. In Buddhist terms this orientation makes the funeral a significant merit-making event for the deceased

Monk chanting at a funeral ceremony

and also for the living, although merit-making and protective magic seem to be closely related in these mortuary rites. Death rites also celebrate the continuance of a social group — family, community, village — thereby mitigating the threat of death to social cohesion and solidarity.

In this chapter we have examined selected facets of Buddhism and society in Southeast Asia on the level of popular belief and practice. We stressed the centrality of master stories or paradigmatic models as the framework for conveying the normative values of the tradition. We then studied two festivals, *Visākhā Pūjā* and *Loi Krathong*, and two rites of passage, monastic ordination and the funeral, as examples of the syncretic nature of popular Buddhism and expressions of the way in which the people of Theravadin Southeast Asian cultures ascribe meaning to their lives through the integration of patterns of sacred history, individual life stages, and the cycles of an agricultural community.

CHAPTER 2

Buddhism, Political Legitimation, and National Integration

IN THE PRECEDING chapter we examined several facets of traditional Theravāda Buddhism in Southeast Asia as they have survived into the modern period. By and large the sociological context for this examination was the village and small town. Resources for this material included my own field work and research by contemporary anthropologists. In the present chapter we shift our attention to a different context, the monarchy and the nation-state, with an appropriate change of themes from ritual, festival, and rites of passage to the Buddha as cosmocrator (i.e., one who establishes the order of the world, who empowers it or makes it sacred), King Aśoka as the paradigmatic ruler, the development of the notion of the God-King, and, finally, the rise of charismatic Buddhist political leaders in the post-colonial period. Resources for this study include the traditional Theravāda Buddhist chronicles of Sri Lanka, Burma, and Thailand, archaeological evidence from such majestic monuments as Borobudur, Angkor, Pagan, and Sukhothai, and modern historical sources. The themes of this chapter have been addressed in both scope and specificity in the past few years by both historians of religion and anthropologists.[44] Audio-visual instructional resources on these subjects are, however, relatively meager. For obvious reasons some do not readily lend themselves to this kind of depiction. Furthermore, as we might expect, those which have been the subject of film studies have generally been related to the ancient monuments constructed under the aegis of powerful Buddhist monarchs.* Be that as it may, no study of Buddhism and society in Southeast Asia would be complete without an exploration of these themes.

*The Government of India has produced several films on some of the great Indian Buddhist sites. They include: *Cave Temples of India* which focuses on Ajanta; *Immortal Stupa* which deals with Sāñcī; *Nalanda* which depicts one of the greatest Buddhist universities; and *Land of Enlightenment*, a brief survey of classical Buddhist sites in Bihar, e.g., Bodhgaya, Sārnāth. The BBC has also produced a film on Sañci (*The Glory That Remains*). Borobudur has been the subject of two films, *Borobudur: The Cosmic Mountain* and *The Buddha. Temple Complex at Borobudur*, as has Angkor, *Angkor. The Ancient City* and *Angkor. The Lost City*. Most of these films are now somewhat dated and generally fail to include the kind of historical and contextual background that would enhance the films' classroom value.

Angkor Wat

A. The Buddha as Cosmocrator

In our earlier examination of the consecration of a Buddha image we saw the crucial significance of the magical power associated with the Buddha. This power manifests iself in several other ways as well. In classical Theravāda texts like the *Mahāparinibbāna Sutta* (The Buddha's Great Decease) we find the themes of the Buddha as teacher and miracle worker interwoven. The cult of Buddha relics and their association with ruling monarchs discussed in this important text bear testimony to the magical power latent in these physical remains of the great teacher. As we shall see, the cult of relics figures prominently in a consideration of this topic. The Buddha as consecrator of the land plays an even more central role, however; that is, the Buddha's physical presence serves to establish a "holy land" (*buddhadesa*). This occurs consistently in Southeast Asian Therāvada chronicles by means of the Buddha's miraculous visits to these regions.

Both the *Island Chronicle* (*Dīpavaṃsa*) and the *Great Chronicle* (*Mahāvaṃsa*) open with an account of the Blessed One's three visits to the Sri Lanka in

Cetiya containing relics of the Buddha

the first eight years of his enlightenment.* As the *Island Chronicle* states in its opening line: "Listen to me. I shall relate the Chronicle of the *Buddha's coming to the island* . . . ." The same pattern emerges in Burmese, Thai, and Laotian chronicles. For example the oldest extant Burmese chronicle, *The Celebrated Chronicle* by SamantapasādikaSīlvavaṃsa (fifteenth century) follows the typical Theravāda chronicle pattern of moving from a discussion

*Of special interest in connection with this discussion is *In the Steps of the Buddha* which uses the Kelaniya Mural depictions (at the Kelaniya Temple outside of Colombo) of the *Dīpavaṃsa's* record of the three visits of the Buddha to Sri Lanka to convert the aboriginals and enshrine Buddha relics, to bring peace to warring factions, and to visit Sumantakuta and Kelaniya.

of the kings of Buddhist India, the Buddhist conquest of Sri Lanka, and then the Buddha's visit to Lekaing village in the Tagaung kingdom of Burma, a story repeated in the famous *Glass Palace Chronicle of the Kings of Burma* commissioned by King Bagyidaw in 1829. This legend has two brothers, Mahapon and Sulapon, making a request of the Buddha to visit their country and building a sandalwood monastery for him: "the Lord foreseeing that in time to come his religion would be established for a long time in Burma, came many times with . . . five hundred saints until the monastery was finished. And when it was finished he gathered alms for seven days, enjoyed the bliss of mystic meditation, and refreshed the people with the ambrosia of his teaching (*dhamma*)."[45] The story goes on to tell of the conversion of 500 men and 500 women to the Buddha's teaching and their attainment of sainthood (*arahat*). By tracing the origin of the establishment of Buddhism in Burma to the Buddha himself, the chronicler not only makes the tradition authoritative but more authoritative than its home of historical origin. As the *Celebrated Chronicle* argues, "in Sri Lanka the religion did not begin to arise before the year A.D. 236 [the date of the conversion of King Devānampīyatissa by Mahinda]. But in our land religion arose since the time the Lord came to dwell in the sandalwood monastery."[46] Thai Buddhist chronicles tell much the same kind of story with miraculous elaborations. In the *Epochs of the Conqueror* it is related that the Buddha took his bowl and robe and flew from Vārāṇasī to Haripuñjaya in northern Thailand where he also preached the *dhamma* and established the people in the three refuges and the five moral precepts.[47] In other chronicles such as *The Buddha Travels the World* (*Phracao Liep Lōk*) the Buddha's visit initiates towns and monasteries, laying out a kind of sacred geography, and the chronicles of major monasteries begin with a founding by the Buddha.

Political units are also built around extensions of the Buddha, namely his relics and his image. When the Buddha made his legendary visit to northern Thailand, for example, he predicted that one of his relics would be discovered by King Ādicca.[48] This discovery coincides with the expansion of the Kingdom of Haripuñjaya and undoubtedly points to royal support for Theravāda Buddhism which served to abet integration of a growing political unit.

The Buddha relic symbolizes political authority in two ways. First, when enshrined in a *cetiya* or reliquary mound it functions as a magical center or *axis mundi* for the kingdom. The enshrined relic or *cetiya* becomes the symbol par excellence of the monarch as *cakkavattin* or "wheel turner." Second, the Theravāda chronicles point to the fact that the Buddha relic is only one religious factor among many being exploited for the purposes of political legitimation and integration. For instance, in the case of Anawratā, who established the Kingdom of Pagan in Burma in the late eleventh century, both the ideology of Theravāda Buddhism as well as the institution of the monastic order figure prominently in his strategy. Other Buddhist symbols of legitimation include the Theravāda scriptures and

Buddha images. The three together — relic, scripture, and image — have been correlated with two aspects of the Buddha nature in the Theravāda tradition (i.e., the *dhammakāya* and the *rūpakāya*) and with two types of guardian deities in Southeast Asia.[49] Hence, these symbols integrate the forces of both Buddhist and nonBuddhist traditions in support of the authority and power of Southeast Asian monarchial traditions which began emerging in Burma, Thailand, Cambodia, and Laos from the end of the eleventh century A.D. We shall look briefly at one of them, the Emerald Buddha, the palladium of the Chakri Dynasty in Thailand, as another example of the power of the Buddha as cosmocrator.*

The story of the origin of the Emerald Buddha image or the Holy Emerald Jewel is told in the northern Thai chronicles as follows:

> Some 500 years after the death of the Buddha the holy monk, Nāgasena, counselor to the famous king Milinda (or Menander), wanted to make an image of the Buddha to propagate the faith. Fearing that an image of gold or silver would be destroyed, he decides to make one from a precious stone endowed with special power. Sakka (i.e., Indra), becoming aware of this wish, goes to Mt. Vibul to obtain a suitable gem from the great *cakkavatti* king or Universal Monarch who has in his possession seven precious stones with supernatural powers. Since only a *cakkavatti* king can possess such a gem, the guardians of Mt. Vibul offer an Emerald Jewel which is of the same essence and comes from the same place as the gem requested by Sakka. The god takes the Emerald Jewel to Nāgasena. Vissukamma, the divine craftsman, then appears in the guise of an artisan and fashions the Jewel into a Buddha image. When it is completed, the holy monk invites the seven relics of the Buddha to enter into it. Finally, he predicts that the image will be worshipped in Cambodia, Burma, and Thailand.[50]

The chronicles then proceed to narrate the story of the image which moves from India to Sri Lanka, Angkor, and various Thai principalities. The Emerald Buddha emerges clearly onto the pages of history in the fifteenth century during the reign of Tilokarājā of Chiang Mai. In the mid-sixteenth century it is taken to Laos where it remained until 1778 when it was brought to Bangkok where it is found today in the chapel of the grand palace, venerated as the protector of the Chakri dynasty.

*This discussion of the image of the Emerald Buddha could be put within the framework of an art historical look at the Buddha image in Thailand or the Buddha image in Buddhist Asia. For the former, *Thai Images of the Buddha* is appropriate, especially when used in conjunction with the catalogue prepared for the exhibit, *The Arts of Thailand*. The broader context could be provided by the slide set, *The Evolution of the Buddha Image*, for which a catalogue was also printed.

There is a great need for a first-class film on a Buddha consecration ceremony as discussed in the preceding chapter. Such a film, or perhaps newly developed slides and other audio-visual materials could then be used with art historical films and slides to study the phenomenon of the Buddha image from both history of religions and art historical perspectives.

The Emerald Buddha possesses a power inherent in the precious stone itself, but its supernatural character is enhanced by the association it had with such cult objects as the Indrakhila, the guardian spirit of the capital city of Chiang Mai, and, moreover, its identification with the *cakkavatti* king or the Buddha in his *cakkavatti* aspect. Possession of the Emerald Buddha endowed a monarch with special power and authority.

> Through the proper veneration of the Jewel the king gained the support of sovereign power in its most potent and beneficent form. And, on a deeper level, the king's meditation on the Jewel imbued him with that power and thereby enabled him to exercise authority, to establish order, and to guarantee the protection for the kingdom. Moreover, it was this identification between the Jewel and the Buddha-Cakkavatti which provided the ultimate justification for one of the most important functions associated with the Jewel in the Thai and Laotian kingdoms where it was venerated — namely, its role as the sovereign ruler before whom the various princes of the kingdom swore their fealty to the reigning monarch who possessed it.[51]

The relationship between the person of the Buddha and political authority has many fascinating symbolic and historical dimensions. The central theme which emerges from the traditional Southeast Asian Theravāda Buddhist chronicles, however, is the power of the Buddha as cosmocrator. The Buddha sacralizes the land, He becomes the ground of political order and power, through his *physical* presence, his actual visitations or symbols of his physical presence, i.e., his relics and his images. Although such a notion may seem antithetical to the statement by the Buddha that only his teachings (*dhamma*) were his legitimate successor, the canonical Pāli texts make abundantly clear there are two "wheels of *dhamma*," the Four Noble Truths and the Eightfold Noble Path outlined in the Buddha's First Discourse, but also the righteous political ruler (*dhammarāja*) with power and authority to order an otherwise chaotic society.[52] In short, the Buddha has two basic aspects: the mundane (*lokiya*) and transmundane (*lokuttara*); the princely and the ascetic; power and compassion. Rather than being antithetical, they are fundamentally interrelated, although not always in the same way. Our examination of the Buddha as cosmocrator opens up one facet of that symbiosus.

B. The God-King (*devarāja*)

The visitor to Southeast Asia who manages to escape the confines of the International Hiltons finds him/herself overawed by some of the most spectacular religious monuments in the world. Among the extant Buddhist remains of monumental size and scope, Borobudur in Java, Angkor in Cambodia, and Pagan in Burma cannot be rivaled. They represent the high points in the development of their respective cultures: the Śailendras, the Khmers, and the Burmans. But to assess them simply as magnificent expressions of powerful, centralized monarchies fails to get beyond an appreciation of their material size. It misses their symbolic value, and also what they can tell us about the interrelationship between Southeast Asian Buddhism and political states from the tenth to the fourteenth centuries. This section of our examination of Buddhism, political legitimation and national integration, will briefly explore these three expressions of cultural genius and creativity. The god-king (*devarājā*) concept unifies their structure and also their intentionality. It should be pointed out, however, that the meaning of this concept is not without dispute.[53] We shall note the main point of this debate, and then move on to a brief examination of Borobudur, Angkor, and Pagan.

In its most simple and extreme formulation the *devarājā* concept stands for the divinization of a ruler; that is, a ruler becomes the apotheosis of a divine being, be it Śiva or Viṣṇu, or of a Buddha like Lokeśvara (Avalokiteśvara). The definitive statement of this position was made by the great French scholar, George Coedès in regard to his studies of Angkor: "From all evidence it is safe to say that it was the king who was the great god of ancient Cambodia, the one to whom the biggest groups of monuments and all the temples in the form of mountains were dedicated."[54] Other formulations are less extreme, claiming that in the case of Hinduism the ruler was considered to be either an incarnation of a god or a descendant from a god or both, and that in the case of Theravāda Buddhism the king became a representative of god, i.e., Indra, through good *karma* acquired through past lives.[55] Such a formulation of the *devarājā* notion has the virtue of allowing for diversity of interpretation. Even Coedès qualifies his extreme position in other writings. The major challenge to this interpretation comes from a few French and German scholars who contend that the *devarājā* concept in Angkor referred to Śiva as the "king of the gods" rather than to a divine monarch (i.e., the god-king).[56] While the historical and philological complexities of the position are beyond the scope of this essay, these scholars basically argue for a separation of the *devarājā* notion from a cult of royal *liṅgas* which became the basis of the Angkorian state cult from the eleventh century onwards.[57] Having noted the focus of the debate we turn now to Borobudur.

Borobudur*

The terraced pyramid known as Borobudur was constructed on the Kedu plain outside of present-day Jogjakarta in the mid-eighth century A.D. by a ruling dynasty who called themselves the Śailendras, or "kings

---

*The two films on Borobudur, *Borobudur: The Cosmic Mountain* and *The Buddha: Temple Complex at Borobudur* differ dramatically. The latter merely utilizes the Borobudur bas-reliefs to present episodes from the life of the Buddha. The former connects this great monument with the past, present, and future of Indonesia, explores the structure and meaning of Borobudur, and puts it within a broad cultural context.

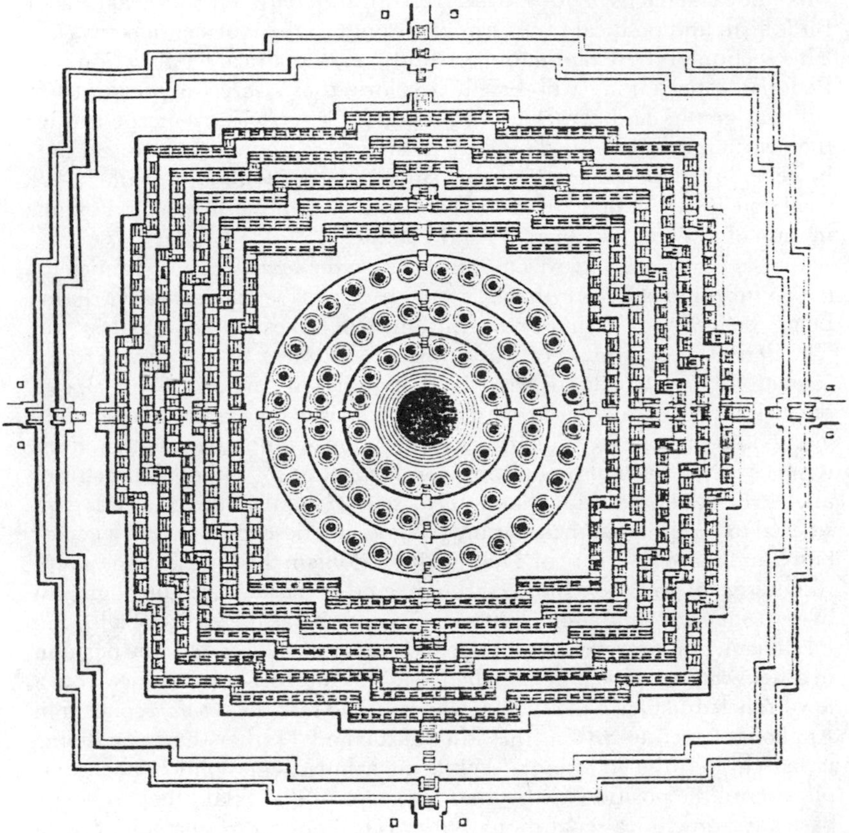

Ground plan of Borobudur

From A. J. Bernet Kempers, *Ancient Indonesian Art.* Harvard University Press, 1959. Used with permission.

of the mountain."[58] The body of the structure consists of six square terraces, the lowest being 479 feet square, topped by three circular platforms bearing 72 perforated, hollow *stūpas* covering seated Buddha images of Vairocana, and a central *stūpa* 52 feet in diameter.[59] The walls of the terraces and the lower basement are covered with bas-reliefs. The ground level portrays the operation of *karma* and rebirth depicting in graphic detail malevolent and beneficent human acts which result in punishments in hell or heavenly rewards. The terraces are preambulation galleries on whose inner walls are depicted the life of the Buddha according to the *Lalita Vistara* and stories from the *Divyāvadāna, Jātakamālā,* and *Gaṇḍāvyuha*. The outer walls of the terraces contain five rows of *dhyani* Buddhas, 92 on each side. The terraced pyramid represents a spiritual ascent from the mundane world of karmic action and rebirth, through encounters with the historical Buddha, and various Mahāyāna Buddhas and *bodhisattvas*:

> The higher we ascend, the wider rises our spiritual horizon . . . At the foot of the monument we contemplate the misery caused by the wheel of life, and the unavoidable inevitable Law of Karma is brought before our eyes in impressive scenes. Following on this, we are shown how the Buddha preached the Law of Salvation, how in this last earthly existence he attained Buddhaship, for which task he qualified himself by many deeds of self-sacrifice through innumerable former existences. Next comes the story of the seeker after the highest Wisdom, the symbolic wanderings of Sudhana.[60]

The pilgrim joins Sudhana on his quest encountering Mañjuśrī and Samantabhadra before emerging at the circular upper galleries, the sphere of the Ādi Buddha Vajrasattva.

Borobudur can be seen in ways other than as mapping stages of an individual journey, however. Paul Mus, for example, has interpreted it as a representation of the upper stages of a cosmic mountain enclosed by the cupola of the sky.[61] As a cosmic mountain or *axis mundi* it serves as a connection with the divine source of royal power, the *dharma* which is the basis of all Buddhas and *bodhisattvas*. But Borobudur also may connect a chthonous cult of "kings of the mountain" with the Ādi-Buddha, the universal Buddha nature. De Casparis has argued that in Śailendra inscriptions the Sanskrit term, *gotra*, was used both to mean the fundamental element of Buddhahood as well as the "line of the ancestors," thereby identifying the family of the Tathāgata with the Śailendra ancestoral line.[62] Borobudur, from this point of view, becomes not only the temple of the Buddha Vairocana but the temple and burial place of Indra Śailendra, its builder.

H. G. Quartich Wales acknowledges that Borobudur symbolizes stages on the Buddhist path to supreme enlightenment and transformation as a *vajrasattva* ("diamond-being"), and that it also represents a staged mountain leading to the root (*mula*) of the dynasty at the top; however, he finds the most striking connections between the stages toward *vajrasattva* perfection, and a shaman's stage by stage ascent through the skies: "Just as the Altai shaman ascends in trance through the various heavens to the presence of Bai Ulgan, now at Borobudur the Buddhist devotee might hope to attain via the various 'steps' in concentrated meditation the final deliverance of Nirvāna."[63]

While interpretations of Borobudur vary, they are not necessarily incompatible or inconsistent. Indeed, it would be surprising if this great monument did not symbolize Indian Buddhist cosmology and metaphysics within the context of the individual's journey to spiritual perfection, and, at the same time integrate these elements with a chthonous ancestoral cult which may have had connections with an indigenous shamanism.

Angkor

Angkor, even more than Borobudur, has caught the imagination of European travelers and scholars, if for no other reason than its overwhelming size and dynamism.* Furthermore, while scholars like Coedès have interpreted Borobudur in terms of the *devarāja* concept, its structure and rich inconography give prominence to its specifically Buddhist and religious significance. Perhaps it was this reason that prompted A. K. Coomaraswamy's comment that in Borobudur, "there is no nervous tension, no concentration of force to be compared with that which so impresses the observer at Angkor Wat.[64] The *devarāja*, however, has had its primary association with Khmer civilization, particularly the development of Angkor, its capital.

The *devarāja* concept probably originated with Funan, a kingdom founded in the first century A.D. in the lower Mekong valley. The Chinese word, *Fu-nan*, is probably derived from the Mon-Khmer, *bnam*, meaning "mountain" with reference to a cult of a national guardian spirit established by the founder of the State.[65] During the Khmer Dynasty it was given specific definition during the reign of Jayavarman II from 802 when Śaivism became the State cult. The central divinity of this cult was the king himself, looked upon as a manifestation of Śiva, hence, a god-king (*devarāja*) whose visible symbol was a *liṅga* set upon the central altar of a pyramidal temple, the symbolic center of the Empire, an imitation of Mount Meru.[66] Jayavarman made his royal chaplain (*hotar*), Śivakaivalya, the chief priest (*purohita*) of the *devarāja* cult on a hereditary basis. This insured continuance of the cult until the reign of Sūryavarman I (A.D. 1002-1050), who added Mahāyāna Buddhism to the state *devarāja* cult. It is known that he built a Buddhist central temple on the site later to become the Bayon, the great temple of Lokeśvara/Jayavarman VII, constructed at the end of the twelfth century. It can be inferred that in the tradition of

*Of the two Angkor films, *Angkor: The Ancient City*, has very limited educational value. Although *Angkor: The Lost City*, is very brief (12 minutes), it does provide an idea of the historical development of the capital, Angkor Thom, the concept of the god-king, and the eclecticism of Khmer religion. The slide set, *L'Art Khmer*, shows many scenes of Angkor.

Angkor Wat

the *devarājā* Sūryavarman became a *buddharājā*, an incarnate Buddha. Such was certainly the case during the reign of Jayavarman VII who, as the Bayon testifies, identified himself with Lokeśvara.

It may well be the case, as W. B. Quartich Wales and others speculate, that the Khmer *devarājā* cult is a synthesis of Indian/Śaivite ideas of divinity and kingship with older Megalithic beliefs in Southeast Asia. When these peoples erected menhirs, they recognized the consubstantial presence of the first ancestor/earth god in the stone as themselves.[67] Wales finds corroboration of the chthonic character of Śiva among the Khmers in such epithets as Girisa, "the mountain Lord," and Gambhireśvara, "Śiva of the depths." He argues that the development of the temple mountain in Khmer architecture up to the Bayon points towards a displacing of the Hindu Meru by a more realistic and primordial representation of the sacred mountain which was a revival of the chthonic source of divine and royal power.[68]

But what of Angkor Wat, the most famous temple of the ancient Khmer empire? Sometimes known as the Great Temple, Angkor Wat covers an area of approximately 500 acres and is part of a large complex of buildings extending over 10,000 acres. It was built by Sūryavarman II (A.D. 1113-1150) and dedicated to the Hindu god Viṣṇu, although later it was used as a temple for both Mahāyāṇa and Theravāda Buddhism as these traditions came to be favored by Khmer monarchs. Angkor Wat is really a walled and moated fortress-palace, the residence of the king, as well as a temple representing the celestial paradise of Viṣṇu.[69] The moat surrounding the structure is about 200 yards wide and 25 feet deep. The temple itself, symbolizing the earth in its quadrangular plan and guarded by two massive walls, rises as Mt. Sumeru, the central mountain of the universe, to the celestial spheres of Viṣṇu-lōka. A bridge crosses the moat on the west, leading through the main gate of the outer wall and gallery. The pilgrim walks across a paved causeway to a cruciform terrace in front of the main entrance to the temple. The temple itself rises in three successive terraces to a height of 65 meters. In the center of the innermost terrace stands an enormous pyramidal basement supporting the five ultimate towers reached by very steep stone stairways.[70]

Angkor Wat and later the capital Angkor Thom with its central temple, the Bayon, can be seen as a magical diagram or *maṇḍala* of the universe. The three essential elements are the central mountain, the ocean (i.e., the moat), and the enclosing mountains (i.e., the wall).[71] Furthermore, by identifying the temple with the monarch the structure not only represented the universe but also the kingdom, thereby uniting religion and the state in common symbol. Finally, Angkor Wat, like Borobudur, also represents an individual journey through levels and galleries representing the mythological worlds of Hinduism to the blessed world of the supreme god Viṣṇu, himself.

*Pagan**

In concluding our examination of the *devarājā* notion an even briefer mention must be made of Pagan, the only one of the three monuments discussed that was predominantly influenced by Theravāda Buddhism. Pagan became the capital of a Burma unified under King Anawratā (1040-1077). Located in central Burma in a plain near the confluence of the Irrawaddy and the Chandwin, the city covered an area of approximately sixteen square miles where the remains of over 5,000 *stūpas* can still be seen. While Pagan lacks the majesty of Angkor and the impressive splendor of Borobudur, its sheer extent is overwhelming. The *stūpas* of Pagan vary greatly in architectural style, reflecting Indian and Mon influences as well as the unique genius of the Burmese. The Shwezigon, begun by Anawratā and later completed by his grandson, Kyanzittha, enshrines three sacred Buddha relics, his collar bone, his frontlet bone, and tooth. It stands in the tradition of the *cetiya* reliquary representing the power and virtue of the *cakkavattin* discussed earlier. Other *stūpas* such as the Shwesandaw and Mingalazedi (A.D. 1274) reflect the basic structure of Borobudur with truncated pyramidal terraced bases with angle towers

*The slide set, *Buddhism*, produced by Kenneth Morgan has slides of Pagan and other important Theravāda sites.

and a central stairway on each side supporting a central circular dome that emerges from the quadrangular base. "The pilgrim is invited to ascend the tower gradually, moving clockwise around its terraces in a symbolic pilgrimage of ascent rising from the ground level of earthly everyday life to higher and higher spheres."[72]

The glory of Pagan, however, is the Ānanda Temple, built by Kyanzittha, who ascended the throne of Pagan in 1084. Made of brick and plaster according to a cruciform plan, the main base is surmounted by two receding curvilinear roofs and four receding terraces, crowned by a spire in the form of a mitre-like pyramid called a *sikhara*.[73] The interior is dominated by an enormous cube which rises to the spire. On each face of the cube a colossal figure of the Buddha stands in the teaching hand posture (*mudrā*). The Ānanda, like the Dhammayangyi Temple and several others, combines both cave and cosmic mountain symbolism. According to the *Glass Palace Chronicle* the temple is a replica of an ascetic's cave located on Mt. Gandamadana in a mythological Himalayan setting. The gilded spire suggests not only the top of a magic mountain but also flames or fiery energy generated by the meditation of the Buddha inside the cave.

That Pagan was situated only thirty miles from Mt. Popa, the home of some of the most powerful guardian spirits (*nats*) worshipped by the Burmese, suggests assimilation between the Mt. Meru symbolism of Indian Buddhist cosmology and an ancient cult of mountain spirits. That an image of Kyanzittha is located inside the temple would appear to corroborate inscriptional claims that he saw himself as a *bodhisattva* and a *cakkavattin* as well as an incarnation of the god Viṣṇu. In the opinion of one interpreter of Southeast Asian culture, Kyanzittha sought to realize his own apotheosis as a divine being in a way similar to that of his contemporaries in Cambodia: "We can . . . see the Ānanda as a funerary temple for Kyanzittha. It represents a model of cosmic reality, a world wherein dwell those who have achieved enlightenment. Kyanzittha has spent his life as a *bodhisattva* and on his death he achieves translation into the realm of the Buddhas."[75]

While the exact nature of the *devarāja* cult in Southeast Asia appears to be variously interpreted, the fact that such monarchs as Indra Śailendra, Jayavarma VII, and Kyanzittha were identified as divine beings or were claimants to divine status served to enhance their own power and authority. The buildings they sponsored did more than glorify their own person, however; they were magical centers for the state as well as the cosmos, and symbolized not only the spiritual attainments of the monarch, but the journey all aspirants to enlightenment and perfection must take. The fragmentation of our own world view undermines our ability to live in such an integrated cosmos, but we can still enter imaginatively into that milieu. To make such a leap demands not that we suspend critical analyses of such cultural marvels, but that they become part of our efforts to understand religion more holistically. Toward that end we urge the use of films such as *Borobudur: The Cosmic Mountain* which place that monument in a broad cultural and historical context.

C. Aśoka. The Exemplary Buddhist Ruler

The Buddhist chronicles of Theravāda Southeast Asia often begin their legendary histories with the Buddha's visit to the country of the chronicle's origin. Before recounting the history of Buddhism in that area and the support particular kings rendered the Buddhist monastic order, they often outline the history of Theravāda Buddhism in India and Sri Lanka. In that account, one monarch particularly stands out, namely, Aśoka Maurya. He becomes the exemplar *par excellence* for all Buddhist monarchs, embodying the virtues of righteousness and justice, supporting the monastic order materially, and ensuring both religious and political harmony within the realm. In effect, the Aśoka paradigm becomes another way of legitimating political authority and integrating a sociopolitical realm. This section will explore some of the ways in which this was done.

Aśoka was the grandson of Chandragupta Maurya, the founder of the Mauryan dynasty. He forged the most far-reaching political unity India was to know until the colonial period, ruling over this vast empire from 270 to 232 B.C. Following the custom of the Persian ruler, Darius the Great, Aśoka set up commemorative rock edicts around his realm. These edicts plus the *Aśoka Avadāna* (The Story of King Aśoka) in Sanskrit and three Pāli works, the *Dīpavaṁsa* (The Island Chronicle), the *Mahāvaṁsa* (The Great Chronicle) and Buddhaghosa's commentary on the *Vinaya* (Book of Discipline) provide us with a significant — although historically problematic — fund of information about this great Indian ruler.

Aśoka's conversion to Buddhism and its consequences becomes the seminal event in the history of Theravāda Buddhism, not simply for the development of Buddhism in India but for the normative value his example has for the way monarchs in the Theravāda cultures of Southeast Asia are perceived. Rulers such as Anawratā of Pagan and Tilokarājā of Chiang Mai do what Aśoka did, or at least the chronicles writing in the Theravāda Mahāvihāra tradition report events in this manner. In following the Aśoka model or in exemplifying the Aśoka paradigm, these rulers not only lend their reign legitimacy and authority in a particular location; they also become part of a more universal history. The religion they support literally has its roots in the person of the Buddha, whose physical presence magically resides in his relics, and their political rule has its roots in the legendary career of Aśoka. What are some of the most salient aspects of the Aśoka narrative?

We begin with Aśoka's conversion to Buddhism. In the ninth year of Aśoka's reign a war broke out between Magadhā and Kaliṅga, perhaps the most powerful kingdom of India still independent of Aśoka's rule. According to a reference in the Thirteenth Rock Edict it was the remorse and pity aroused in his mind by the horrors of the conquest — the killing, death by disease, the forcible dislocation of noncombatants including monks and priests — that resulted in his conversion. He came to the opinion that the only true conquest was not by force of arms but by the force of religion (*dhamma*). Just exactly what this *dhamma* was is a matter of some debate. The legends in the chronicles make him an active patron of the monastic order, the convenor of the Third Buddhist Council which purged the *saṅgha* of 60,000 heretics, a promoter of the Buddha's teachings, and the claim that in his old age he became a monk. The *dhamma* of the Rock Edicts, however, presents an idealistic, humanitarian philosophy with little doctrinal concern for Buddhism. Aśoka advocates docility to parents, liberality to friends, economy in expenditures and avoiding of disputes (Rock Edict 3). He urges self-mastery, purity of heart, gratitude, and fidelity (Rock Edict 7). Like the *Sigālovāda Sutta* to which the *dhamma* of the Rock Edicts is sometimes likened, Aśoka advises right conduct toward servants, honor towards teachers, liberality to Brahmins and recluses, and self-restraint toward all living things (Rock Edicts 9 and 11). His moral advice is inspiring but not necessarily specifically Buddhist:

> Man sees but his good deeds, saying: "This good act have I done." Man sees not all his evil deeds, saying: "That bad act have I done, that act is corruption." Such self-examination is hard. Yet, must a man watch over himself, saying: "Such and such acts lead to corruption, such are brutality, cruelty, anger, and pride. I will zealously see to it that I slander not out of envy. That will be to my advantage in this world, to my advantage, verily, in the world to come."[76]

Nevertheless, there can be little doubt that Aśoka was influenced by Buddhist teachings, that he did support the monastic order, and that his conversion offers a paradigmatic parallel to the exemplary model of the Buddha.

It is informative to compare the structure of the Buddha and Aśoka legends. Above all, the Buddha's life-story exemplifies the movement from a modality characterized by ignorance and attachment to one of freedom and knowledge. Even though the one (*nibbāna*) overcomes the other (*saṁsāra*), the two presuppose each other; and, in this sense, are necessarily interdependent. In a similar manner Aśoka's life story moves between the poles of cruelty, wickedness, and disorder (*Candāsoka*) and justice, righteousness, and order (*Dhammāsoka*). This same polarity is evident in two Pāli Sutta texts which treat kingship, the *Aggañña Suttanta* and the *Cakkavatti Sīhanāda Suttanta*. The first justifies the selection of a king, "the great elect" (*mahāsammata*) as a necessary means to overcome political, economic and social disorder brought about by human greed and avarice.[77] The second "... presents two apocalyptic images — of life under the rule of evil and of life ruled by *dhamma*. The one is a picture of injustice, disorder, and confusion; the other portrays liberation and reciprocity. Both are extended images of the human potential, kept in balance as with Aśoka. From the Buddhist standpoint, neither one can be fully appreciated except in relationship to the other."[78]

The narratives of some of the great Southeast Asian Buddhist monarchs embody the same polarity. Anawratā kills his brother to become the ruler of Pagan and then becomes a patron of Theravāda Buddhism; Tilokarājā revolts against his father, the King of Chiang Mai, before his patronage of the Mahāvihāra sect of Theravāda Buddhism; Duṭṭhagāmaṇī, the hero of the *Mahāvaṁsa* destroys the Tamils, unites the island kingdom of Sri Lanka and then builds many of the great religious edifices of Poḷonnāruva including the Lohapāsāda and the great *stūpa*. The Aśoka legend exemplifies more than a paradoxical bipolarity, however. It inspired the monarchs of Southeast Asia to contribute lavishly to the monastic order. Also following Aśoka's model, monarchs like Tilokarājā convened councils both for the purification of the *dhamma*, i.e., a new redaction of the Pāli scriptures, and to meditate sectarian differences. Finally, they built *stūpa* reliquaries which symbolized the center of their kingdoms and before which other rulers pledged their fealty.

The most famous Buddhist *stūpa*-reliquary, which became the inspiration for the spread of this architectural structure in Southeast Asia and the cult of relics associated with it, is Sāñcī in India, associated with King Aśoka.* According to Sukumar Dutt the prevalence of *stūpa* worship was one of the marks of the cultural unity of the 200-year period from 270-50 B.C., the age of the late Mauryas, the Śuṅgas, and the late Andhras of the south. The association of Sāñcī with Aśoka was inferred from an inscribed Aśokan pillar thought to have originally stood at the south gate.[79] Tradition has it that Aśoka built *stūpa*-reliquaries all over India, 84,000 in all, and while such a figure is fictional, its symbolic value points to a basic truth, namely, that in the Aśokan period the cult of relics became a fundamental expression of Buddhist piety. Indeed, it is thought that the inauguration of the cult of relics in the *Mahāparinibbāna Sutta* may well be a product of the Mauryan age and represents a justification of a practice which had already become popular.[80] If such an interpretation has merit, it suggests that the worship of *stūpas* was, in fact pre-Buddhist, originally being a kind of mound worship or the worship of the remains of rulers interred in large mounds of earth and brick.

Sāñcī is part of a central Indian group of *stūpas*, which includes Bhārhut and Bhilsa along a commercial trunk route from the imperial capital Pāṭaliputra to Ujjain and on to the seaport town of Bharukacha. The typical *stūpa* of which Sāñcī offers one of the most perfect types was composed of three major parts: a mound or dome (*aṇḍa*), a raised platform above the base of the dome for circumambulation (*medhi*), and a stone balustrade (*vedikā*) at ground level encircling the mound. Gateways (*toraṇas*) were

*Since some of the earliest Buddhist monuments in India date from the time of Aśoka, a general film on Buddhist sites, *Land of Enlightenment*, might be used followed by *The Glory That Remains* (also known under the title, *Sermons in Stone*) which explains the pillars of Aśoka, the *stūpas*, railings and gateways of Sāñcī. *Immortal Stupa* (14 minutes) focuses almost exclusively on the reliefs on the four gateways at the cardinal directions around the *stupa*, and could be used at the end of this sequence if considerable attention were to be paid to Sāñcī and to King Aśoka.

located in the balustrade at the four cardinal points. A quadrangular terrace (*harmikā*) was added to the top of the dome over which was placed a parasol of imperial power (*chatra*). The four gateways at the cardinal directions indicate the cosmic symbolism of the *stūpa*, as do the terms for the dome, *aṇḍa* meaning "egg," and *garbha* meaning "womb," which contained the "seed" (*bīja*), i.e., the relic.[81] In addition to this basic architectural structure, the three Sāñcī *stūpa* sites abound in stone sculpture and decorative relief carving, much of which represents scenes from the former lives of the Buddha (*jātaka* tales) and folk themes. Such a proliferation of popular art prompted Sukumar Dutt to see the *stūpa* and the cult associated with it a "vulgarization" of the tradition: "Shuffling somehow out of the precocity of monkish learning, the religion has taken on a popular aspect. It seems to find in this age a new, perhaps a little 'vulgarised,' expression in its unclerical ritualistic worship, in its motives of art, in attitudes of mind and spirit, often at odds with the approved system of the religion."[82]

Heinrich Zimmer provides us with a different interpretation of the Buddhist *stūpa*-reliquary. He sees the *stūpa* as a marriage between the highest ideals of Buddhism and local folk religion: ". . . on the gates and railings, we find a thronging world of forms. Their joyous yet respectful animation is the counterpole to the unembellished quiet of the surface of the dome, illustrating the opposition of *saṁsāra* and *nirvāṇa*."[83] Far from being a vulgarization of the tradition, he argues that the ". . . *stūpa* and its form became the highest symbol of the Buddhist faith. It represented the essence of enlightenment, transcendental reality, *nirvāṇa*. Instead, therefore, of remaining simply a reliquary memorial filled with sacred bones, ash, or crumbled wood, the silently eloquent structure became a signal of man's goal and of the Buddha's attainment.[84] While Zimmer may wax overly eloquent abut the meaning of the *stūpa*, Dutt's conception of the *stūpa* as an expression of popular piety seems to draw too sharp a line between monastic and lay Buddhism, between Buddhism's highest ideals and popular practice. Perhaps the truth lies somewhere between these two interpretations.

Earlier we pointed out that the Buddhist monarchs of Southeast Asia enshrined Buddha relics in *stūpas* (known as *dagobas*, i.e., *dhātu-garbha*, in Sri Lanka, and *cedi*, i.e., *cetiya* in Thailand), and that these *stūpas* represented a magical or supernatural center for the kingdom. In this interpretation the reliquary mound becomes one modality of the Buddha as cosmocrator, one closely associated with the monarch as world ruler. *Stūpas*, however, not only enshrine the relics of the Buddha or Tathāgata but other classifications of holy persons, i.e., *pacceka-buddha* and *tathāgata-sāvaka*, and, more importantly, of the ruler (*cakkavatti-rājā*). The *Mahāparinibbāna Sutta* makes reference to the *stūpa* of a "person-of-dhamma/king-of-dhamma" (*dhammika dhammarājā*), an apparent allusion to King Aśoka.[85] The stupa-reliquary, then, can be seen as the symbol *par excellence* of the traditional Buddhist ruler in Southeast Asia, and the essential interrelationship between religion and the state. We turn now for a brief look at contemporary forms of Buddhism, political legitimation and national integration.

D. National Leaders and Buddhist Charisma

Traditional religion has played a crucial role in the modern histories of many of the so-called developing countries. One of the most dramatic recent examples has been the Islamic countries of the Middle East but also Southeast Asia, i.e., Indonesia and Malaysia. In the post-World War II period Gandhi tapped the rich reservoir of Indian religio-cultural values in the service of his independence movement, and Buddhism has figured importantly in the contemporary political histories of Sri Lanka, Burma, and Thailand. Recent political events in Laos and Cambodia make the future of Buddhism in those countries clouded at best. Given the close identification between Buddhism and the traditional cultures of western dominated countries like Burma and Sri Lanka we should not be surprised to find Buddhism being exploited for the purposes of legitimating nationalistic political forces and new forms of national integration under indigenous leadership. U Nu of Burma and S.W.R.D. Bandaranaike of Sri Lanka provide the most striking examples of political leaders in the post-colonial period who exemplify the Buddhist traditions of the "ruler of *dhamma*" (*dhammika dhammarājā*).

In January 1948 U Nu became the first Prime Minister of the newly independent Union of Burma. He espoused a political ideology which blended Buddhism and socialism.* In essence it was based on the theory that a national community could be built only if the individual members were able to overcome their own selfish interests. U Nu argued that material goods were meant not to be saved or used for comfort but to provide for the necessities of life in the journey to Nirvāṇa.[86] He contended that property and class distinctions should be transcended in the spirit of Buddhist self-abnegation for the good of the larger community. Not unlike the *dhamma* of Aśoka, U Nu espoused an ideology of a welfare state rooted in a *cakkavattin's* superior knowledge about the casuality of deliverance from suffering (*dukkha*) directed toward the humanitarian ideal of the benefit of all sentient beings. He preached a socialistic doctrine of a classless society without want in which all members would strive for moral and mental perfection in order to overcome the constant rounds of rebirth (*saṁsāra*).[87]

While U Nu's political ideology was a blend of Buddhism and socialism, his personal lifestyle embodied elements of the traditional ideal of the Buddhist righteous monarch. Approximately six months after he had taken office an insurrection nearly toppled the government. His response

*In connection with this discussion of U Nu, it would be illuminating to use the film, *Burma, Buddhism and Nationalism*, in which U Nu appears discussing Buddhism and the importance of Buddhism to Burma's national integrity.

to that threat was to take a vow of sexual abstinence so that by the power of his personal example the insurgents would be defeated: "On July 20, 1948, when the insurrection was causing anxiety, I went into my prayer room and before the Holy Image took the vow of absolute purity, making a wish at that time that if I kept that vow the insurgents would be confounded."[88] U Nu created a Buddhist Sāsana Council in 1950 to propagate Buddhism and supervise monks, appointed a minister of religious affairs and ordered government departments to dismiss civil servants thirty minutes early if they wished to meditate. Like King Aśoka he called a Buddhist council to "purify the *dhamma*" and produce a new redaction of the Pāli canon. For that council he constructed a large *stūpa* and assembly hall at the cost of six million dollars, like the kings of old performing meritorious acts on the behalf of the Buddhist sangha. U Nu's overthrow in 1962 at the hands of Ne Win may have come in part from his undue emphasis of Buddhism as the basis of national identity. The modern nation state of Burma contains sizable nonBuddhist and nonBurman minorities, e.g., the Shan, Karen, Chin, who resisted his policies. Furthermore, Donald E. Smith may be correct when he suggests that U Nu escaped from the hard requirements of political leadership through his many religious activities, and that his continual preoccupation with religious matters robbed him of a rational approach to political, economic and social problems.[89] Nevertheless, U Nu represents a modern approximation of the traditional Theravāda Buddhist ideal of the righteous monarch.

Another example of this ideal is S.W.R.D. Bandarnaike, elected Prime Minister of Ceylon (Śri Lanka) in 1956. Like Nu, Bandaranaike exploited the symbols and institutional power of Buddhism to come into office, and it was these same forces which provoked severe communal strife and eventually led to his assassination engineered by a disgruntled Buddhist monk. Despite this consequence, "a prominent feature of the movement led by Bandaranaike consisted in the large-scale participation of Buddhist monks in the political struggle, and there can hardly be any doubt that approval by the Saṅgha was a major factor in legitimizing the political actions taken by him in terms of the living Buddhist tradition of Ceylon."[90]

Like U Nu, Bandaranaike espoused an ideology of Buddhist socialism. As he put it in a speech before the World Fellowship of Buddhists in 1950,

> I believe in democracy because I believe in the Buddhist doctrine, that a man's worth should be measured by his own merit and not some extraneous circumstance and also that human freedom is a priceless possession. The Buddha preached that ultimate freedom of man when the human mind need not be subject even to the will of God, and man was free to decide for himself what was right or wrong . . . . In economics I consider myself a Socialist, for I cannot reconcile, with the spirit of the doctrine of Maitreya, man-made inequalities that condemn a large section of our fellowmen to poverty, ignorance and disease.[91]

In his personal lifestyle Bandaranaike did not symbolize the righteous monarch ideal in the same way as U Nu. Still, there can be no doubt that his justification for both his democratic political beliefs and socialistic economic philosophy rested in Buddhism. He attempted to fashion a Middle Way ideology that was neutralist in international policy and uniquely Sinhalese in national policy. In the eyes of many Sinhalese Buddhists, Bandaranaike is a national hero who stands with the Anagārika Dharmapāla as one of the two great leaders in the modern period who, like the ancient kings, Duṭṭagāmaṇi and Parākramabāhu I, sought to establish the sway of Buddhism over Sri Lanka.

In this chapter we have demonstrated some of the ways in which political authority and power in Southeast Asia have been grounded in Theravāda Buddhism. In the last chapter we saw how central the person of the Buddha was to the rituals, rites and festivals of popular Buddhism. In this context the Buddha as cosmocrator plays an equally central role. We also examined the seminal concept of the god-king (*deva-rāja*) and its expressions in the classical religio-political centers of Borobudur, Angkor and Pagan. Finally, we saw how sacred history came into play in the context of the monarchial state in the form of the paradigmatic, righteous ruler, King Aśoka, and how leaders of independence movements in Burma and Sri Lanka consciously sought to legitimate their new nation states through the symbols and ideology of Theravāda Buddhism.

CHAPTER 3

Modernization. The Challenge of Tradition and Change

RELIGIOUS TRADITIONS are not static. They respond to social, economic, and political change; indeed, they help to shape such change. They challenge alien ideologies and, in doing so, are influenced by them. In stable

Monks on morning food donation rounds

periods of history, religious traditions seem to change only imperceptibly, but in more volatile times the disruption and transformation of religious institutions and ideologies keeps pace with and sometimes outstrips changes in other areas of life. The past two decades have been relatively unstable ones in Southeast Asia, dramatized by political revolution, the overthrow of colonially shaped governments and economies, and the rapid erosion of many traditional institutions, including religion.

Novice receiving morning food donations

The most extreme case in point is Cambodia which seems caught in the paroxysms of a national genocide. In the Cambodian case, the consequences for religious institutions have been disastrous. Therāvada Buddhism as an institution has been effectively eliminated. In Laos the nature of the Buddhist *saṅgha* has been drastically altered, but it still survives. The future of Theravāda Buddhism in both of these countries seems to be problematical at best. While contemporary challenges to traditional Theravāda Buddhism have not been as severe in Burma, Thailand, and Sri Lanka, there have been deep strains, and institutional Buddhism has had to adapt in various ways. This chapter will examine the nature of some of these changes, whenever possible shaping the discussion in relationship to available audio-visual resources.* The themes we shall explore will be the changing roles of the monk and the laity.[92]

*Films on this topic are the least adequate of the three areas discussed in this essay. The challenge which modernization poses to the *saṅgha* is suggested at the end of *Buddhism: Be Ye Lamps Unto Yourselves*. In a sequence depicting a monk going out of the monastery to meet with what appears to be a group of civil servants, *Temple of the Pagodas* hints at some of the changes taking place in the Thai *saṅgha*. *Thailand*, shown on public television as one of the *Views of Asia* series, includes one of the longest sequences dealing specifically with the monastic order's response to the challenges of today. Finally, there are a few slides in the American Academy of Religion set, *Buddhism in Southeast Asia and Ceylon* (Nos. 139-148) which relate to issues of modernization discussed in this chapter.

A. The Changing Role of the Monk

To what degree has the role of the monk in Theravāda Buddhist Southeast Asia changed, and to what extent has the change been merely in the circumstances surrounding it? This question offers no easy answer and is debated by both adherents and scholars of Buddhism. Monks seem to be engaged in a range of activities heretofore seen as outside legitimate monastic activity. They provided leadership in the early independence movements in Burma and Sri Lanka in the first decades of this century. Vietnamese monks protested the corrupt Diem regime through dramatic acts of self-immolation, and a balanced historical-political analysis of the Vietnam war, *Lotus in a Sea of Fire*, was written by a monk, Thich Nhat Hahn.[93] In the early 70s Thai monks became politically active on both the left and the right.

Buddhist monks in Southeast Asia have taken part in a wide range of activities with both direct and indirect political consequences. On the surface such involvement seems antithetical to the traditional apolitical role of the Theravāda monk. Or is it? Although the monastic order provides an alternative to the householder's pursuit of mundane goals, it has never been isolated from politics: Monks have been advisors to and have tried to influence political leaders, and we have examined some aspects of the symbiotic relationship between traditional monarchies and the monastic order in the last chapter. Indeed, by its very existence the monastery unavoidably participates in a political order. Contemporary monks have justified political activism on the grounds of both historical precedent and sociological inevitability. Nevertheless, the form of political involvement has obviously changed from the days of absolute monarchies.[94]

Today if monks are perceived as political actors, or as performing roles that are basically secular rather than religious, they run the risk of undermining the symbolic status of the monastic order. In Sri Lanka we have the dramatic example of a disgruntled monk being held responsible for the assassination of S. W. R. D. Bandaranaike, the Prime Minister. In more general terms, a letter to the monthly publication of the Colombo Young Men's Buddhist Association put the problem this way:

> . . . the Buddhist public are naturally embarrassed and dismayed to find bhikkhus in vehicles, with briefcases tucked under their arms, looking quite brisk and business-like, meticulously handling money, haunting shops, cinemas and public places, with all the materialistic fervor of dedicated worldlings.[95]

Whether or not the symbolic status of the monk is jeopardized depends on both the kinds of activities monks engage in and the way in which they engage them. Monks who are perceived as self-serving and as having worldly goals will inevitably lose the respect of both monks and laity whether they are carrying out traditional roles or fashioning new ones.* By way of contrast, monks who personally embody the ideals of Buddhism and who speak to issues of a political nature with the authority of dhammic insight, will probably retain the respect and win the admiration of their monastic peers and thoughtful laypersons. Although illustrations of these two types could be found in all Theravāda cultures, we shall look at two examples from Thailand: Bhikkhu Kitthivuḍḍho and Bhikkhu Buddhadāsa.[96]

Bhikkhu Kitthivuḍḍho

Bhikkhu Kitthivuḍḍho was born in 1936 and was ordained in 1957. Very early in his monastic career he proved himself to be an able public speaker and administrator. He established a foundation for the study and propagation of Buddhism at one of the major Bangkok monasteries, and opened a school for novices and monks located about 100 kilometers from Bangkok in Chonburi Province. Between the politically volatile years of 1973-1976 which were racked by two massive student demonstrations, Kitthivuḍḍho began speaking out on political issues and even helped to lead a political demonstration of sorts in Bangkok. His stance was generally in strong support of the government. His speeches and writings were anti-communist and critical of radical groups and social disruption. He was identified with a rightwing political movement known as the *Navaphala*.

In a speech on August 16, 1975 entitled, *Sing Ti Khuan Kham Nu'ng* ("Things We Should Reflect On") he argued for national unity in the face of divisiveness at home and threats from across Thailand's borders. He called for support of the government, obedience to the law, and he criticized disruptive tactics by radicals. In particular he offered three solutions to the political and social problems faced by Thai society: the practice of moral virtues (*sīla*), the training of the mind, and the attainment of knowledge (*paññā*). On the surface these solutions seem to be typical of Theravāda Buddhism, but Kittivuḍḍho gave these three teachings a uniquely nationalistic interpretation.

Sīla is referred to in general terms by Kitthivuḍḍho as the five precepts which every Buddhist is expected to follow, e.g., not to take the life of a sentient being, and so on. Kitthivuḍḍho emphasized the prohibition against lying, especially with the intent to sow the seeds of dissention. For the individual, *sīla* means being morally pure and avoiding wrong doing, but on the level of society Kitthivuḍḍho interpreted *sīla* as the law of the nation. If everyone has *sīla*, concluded the monk, they will obey the law and there will be peace and civil order.[97]

Training the mind means, in Kitthivuḍḍho's interpretation, to have a firm or steadfast mind, one that is loyal to the country and does not easily

*Slides of the Supreme Patriarch of the Thai Buddhist *saṅgha* getting out of his canary yellow Mercedes Benz to officiate at the opening of a Chinese department store in Bangkok suggest the kind of monastic activity that provokes criticism by sensitive, liberal Buddhists. See *Buddhism in Southeast Asia and Ceylon*.

waver and bend in the winds of this ideology and that. The practice of mindfulness takes on a practical, political orientation; similarly for wisdom (*paññā*). The problems of Thailand today, he stressed, stem from lack of mutual understanding. Citizens do not understand their duties and responsibilities to society or the causes of the problems they face. Only by such understanding can the people correct social ills and build a happy, peaceful and orderly nation. Kitthivuḍḍho then concluded his talk with an appeal to the major symbols of national unity, "nation, religion, king" as represented by the three colors (red, white and blue) of the Thai flag. "The Buddha taught us," stated the monk, "that whenever we are frightened we should look at the flag and have steadfast hearts."[98]

In July of 1976 Kitthivuḍḍho addressed an audience of government and religious leaders at the college he had founded. This address was an elaboration of an interview with a liberal Thai magazine, *Caturāt*, in which Kitthivuḍḍho developed his ideas about the role of the monk in the context of the political crisis brought about by the student-led revolution of 1973, the creation of a parliamentary system of government in Thailand, and the communist victories in Laos, Cambodia and Vietnam.[99] In the speech entitled, "Killing Communists Is Not Demeritorious," he marshalled several arguments to justify his claim that it would not produce negative *karma*, i.e., suffering in this life or some future life, to kill communists. In his interview he had stated that since communists are against the nation, the religion, and the king, they are subhuman and so to kill them is like killing Satan (*Māra*).[100] Furthermore, he argued that the merit accrued from protecting the nation, the religion and the monarchy was greater than the demerit from taking the life of a communist.

In his speech, later printed as a pamphlet by his Foundation, Kitthivuḍḍho reiterated his statement that soldiers who kill communists gain more merit for protecting the nation, the religion, and the king than the demerit from taking life. Citing the Buddha and scripture as authority for his position, he argued that some people are so hopeless that they are not worth saving and that to kill them is, in fact, to kill *kilesa* (impurity).[101] Killing Communists is like getting rid of impurity and the ideology responsible for the horrible annihilation of millions of people in China, Laos and Cambodia, he asserted.[102] In addition to these arguments Kitthivuḍḍho cited the scriptural criteria constituting an infraction of the first precept, i.e., not to take life: the being must be alive, knowledge that the being has life, intent to kill, acting in order to kill, and death. Kittivuḍḍho argued that those who kill with the *intention* of protecting the nation, the religion, and the king, do not meet the necessary conditions that constitute taking the life of a living being.

Kitthivuḍḍho has been the center of considerable controversy. He tends to be supported by conservative, right-wing political groups and criticized by political liberals and thoughtful Buddhist laypersons who argue that he has subverted the *dhamma* for political purposes. His personal life has also come under attack, most notably that he has been involved in shady car deals. On the basis of such stories in the popular press, he earned the nickname, Kitthi-*Volvo* (after the Volvo car). Whatever the truth of such claims, Kitthivuḍḍho's politicization of the *dhamma* and his own personal example contribute to an undermining of the symbolic status of the monk in Thailand.

Bhikkhu Buddhadāsa

Bhikkhu Buddhadāsa stands in stark contrast to a monk like Kitthivuḍḍho.* Born in 1906 and ordained at 21 he soon rose to become abbot of a historically important monastery in Chaiya, southern Thailand. Not at ease with this administrative position, he established a forest hermitage about four kilometers outside the town with living quarters for approximately fifty monks. All of the residents live in adequate but simple wooden huts and engage in some form of manual labor such as the construction of replicas of bas-reliefs from ancient Indian Buddhist sites. When his health permits, he lectures at the hermitage and in earlier years would speak annually at universities and other professional gatherings. Most of these talks have been recorded and now have been printed as a series of collected works.[103]

In the past few years Buddhadāsa has addressed such topics as "The Kind of Political Reform that Creates Problems," "A Socialism That Can Help the World," and "Democratic Socialism." Unlike Kitthivuḍḍho who seems to subordinate Buddhist *dhamma* to the interests of Thai nationalism, Buddhadāsa offers a political view based on the central Buddhist teachings of nonattachment and dependent co-arising (*paṭicca samuppāda*). He interprets dependent co-arising to mean a situation of mutual balance, a whole composed of interconnected, mutually influencing and mutually influenced parts. On the level of the individual it means that one acts in a nonattached manner on behalf of the whole or on behalf of others. This leads to a middle way ethic of sufficiency, adequacy, appropriateness and normalcy, i.e., not in excess. When this concept is applied to politics we have what Buddhadāsa characterizes as a "spiritual politics," the proper balance of man to man, acting for the interests of the whole. In more practical terms, spiritual politics is a kind of socialism, or to use the Thai term, a "fellowship of restraint" (*saṅgha-niyama*). As an economic system, Buddhadāsa contends, socialism is inherently better than capitalism because it is less acquisitive and competitive.[104] Yet, modern socialism is too materialistic. A spiritual socialism would be rooted in the practice of truth (*sīla-dhamma*). Its governing principles would be working for the best balance of the good of each. No policy in one area would be isolated from policy

***Buddhism in Southeast Asia and Ceylon* has a few slides of Buddhadāsa and his center in southern Thailand. The main building of the center, a "Spiritual Theater," contains a fascinating collection of paintings and murals taken from different religious traditions depicting the themes of attachment and non-attachment. Buddhadāsa and his hermitage are deserving of a film devoted exclusively to his teaching and its embodiment in the center he has created.

matters in other areas. Take the problem of overpopulation, for example. Buddhadāsa argues that population growth must be seen in relationship to resource use, production and distribution. He contends that the earth can stand an even larger population than it now has, but only if there is a better balance among production, distribution, and use. Buddhadāsa concludes that Buddhism's contribution to spiritual politics is to help people see the fundamental interrelatedness of things (i.e., their *paṭicca-samuppāda* nature).

Most Thais, claims Buddhadāsa, think that the highest principles of Buddhism demand that one separate oneself from the world. Such is not the case. The principles of *nirvāna* (i.e., non-attachment) are for everyone because (1) the state of nonattachment was our original state and (2) one we strive to recover from our present unsatisfactory (*dukkha*) condition: "To be non-attached means to be in one's true or original condition – free, at peace, quiet, non-suffering, totally aware."[105] While some may think that this teaching is more appropriate for the monk than the layperson, says Buddhadāsa, the opposite is the case. Lay people are usually more harried than the monk: "Those who are hot and bothered need to cool off. For this reason the Buddha meant the teaching about emptiness (*suññatā*) as the basis for the action of ordinary people."[106] Indeed, in Buddhadāsa's view, emptiness and nonattachment are at the basis of a truly socialistic society where people work for the benefit of the whole and overcome their acquisitive interests.

In the thought and example of Bhikkhu Buddhadāsa we see an attempt to emulate the highest teachings of Buddhism and to apply them to the organization of the body politic in order to promote interpersonal and civic wellbeing. He urges a political involvement based on dhammic insight which sees all forms of political, social, and economic organization not as ends in themselves but as serving spiritual goals. Buddhadāsa may be criticized for being hopelessly idealistic, but then, is that not a more appropriate posture for a religious spokesman than the kind of chauvanistic nationalism of a Bhikkhu Kitthivuḍḍho?

Monks and Community Development

Theravāda monks in Southeast Asia today have become politicized, some in ways consonant with the teachings of Buddhism, others less obviously tied to the moorings of the tradition. The range of their involvement in the issues and problems of their respective countries extends far beyond the political realm, however. In Thailand, Burma, and Sri Lanka they are actively participating in programs of rural and urban uplift and social welfare.* As with their political involvement some of these programs seem more appropriate to the normative teachings of the tradition

* *Thailand* has a sequence of an abbot exhorting his followers to work hard for modernization, and monks attending classes acquainting them with government and private social welfare institutions. A few slides in *Buddhism in Southeast Asia and Ceylon* show monks "graduating" from a development training program in Chonburi, Thailand.

than others and the nature of the monk's activity less detrimental to the symbolic value of the position of the monk. The same general question posed earlier applies to monastic sponsorship of and involvement in various development and welfare programs. As one student of Theravāda Buddhism put it:

> Formerly the monk had been, ideally and often actually, a community leader — educator, sponsor of cooperative work activities, personal and social counselor, and ethical mentor — in the nearly static traditional village. Now, if he is to "resume" such a role, he would have to become at least modestly competent in a whole range of "modern" activities, such as literacy campaigns, modern and technical education, agricultural extension and "community development." . . . All of these are activities designed to generate social and cultural dynamism as well as economic change. The important thing to grasp here is that there is some considerable difference between the essentially conservative "traditional role" of the monk in the traditional village and any credible community leadership role today; for many of the activities now proposed are of a radically different character from those to which a monk sometimes gave leadership a century ago.[107]

The remainder of this section will focus on a community development training program sponsored by the two universities for Buddhist monks in Thailand. We should point out, however, that in recent years social service programs involving monks have also been organized in Laos, Burma, and Sri Lanka. In Burma projects have been sponsored by the Buddha Sāsana Council.[108] In Sri Lanka there have been such organizations as the Ceylon Farmers' Association with the general aim of providing "for the spiritual and material welfare of the people of Ceylon through the island through the medium of the Saṅgha dedicated to the service of mankind and the welfare of the country."[109] Finally, in Thailand the number of relatively significant programs bears testimony to the strength of the *saṅgha* and its close connection with the government.

The Project for Encouraging the Participation of Monks in Community Development was begun in 1966 under the sponsorship of the two Buddhist universities for Thai monks, and by 1973 had run three training sessions for approximately 250 monk-trainees. The 1973 program focused on the metropolitan area of Bangkok and its environs, an area posing particularly pressing problems for the 450 monastery-temples (*wats*) and the monks inhabiting them. The training program had three main purposes: to improve *saṅgha* administration in urban areas, to promote knowledge about the conditions and problems of society, and to investigate ways in which the *saṅgha* could contribute to the solution of the problems faced by urban society.

The main justification given for the monastic training programs in community development sponsored by the two Buddhist universities was based on the premise that the central role played by the *saṅgha* in Thai society in the past is in danger of deteriorization. In modern times society has changed, but the *saṅgha* has not, the program leaders contended. Phra Mahachai, a chief administrator of the 1973 training program observed that traditionally Buddhism was at the heart of Thai society, but presently the role of the *saṅgha* is being seriously questioned. He cited two main reasons for this development: (1) changes in society have caused people to desert Buddhism and its essential values; (2) secular institutions have made adjustments and improvements in recent times whereas the monastic order as an institution has not changed significantly and has, consequently, declined in the estimation of the people.[110] The solution, argued Phra Mahachai, is for the monastic order to recognize its role in Thai society: that its responsibilities extend beyond the confines of the monastery and monastery-related activities into the daily lives of the people.

What have been some of the results of the Project for Encouraging the Participation of Monks in Community Development? Obviously a number of monks have been engaged in a formal study of subjects in which they had been previously untrained. A constant theme of the monks reporting on the benefits derived from the training program was the value of the knowledge gained.[111] This knowledge has, in turn, been put to use in meetings of various kinds organized in the home districts of monks graduating from the training program. The meetings have also borne practical fruit. New buildings on monastery compounds have been constructed, wells have been dug, new roads have been built, dams have been constructed, irrigation channels made, and public health programs have been encouraged. In most cases the presence of the monk has provided the main motivation and guidance for the work. The monk himself, with certain exceptions, has not engaged in actual labor on the project. It is especially important to note that the work being done by the lay person on such projects led by monks is perceived as being religiously as well as practically efficacious. In other words, labor was perceived as meritorious because it was encouraged by the person symbolizing the source of merit, namely, the monk. Although the form of the monk's activity was different, the reciprocal structure of the relationship between the monk and the laity remained intact. This relationship is more difficult to maintain when the monk steps outside of traditionally defined roles, however.

The fundamental issue at stake regarding the involvement of the Buddhist monastic order in rural uplift, social welfare, and community development is whether its symbolic value will be seriously undermined. Although the *saṅgha* has never been "other-worldly" its teachings and disciplines have set it apart as a vocation distinct from mundane vocations. The monk has sought transcendent (*lokuttara*) and not worldly (*lokiya*) goals. For this reason, the *saṅgha* has been perceived as a mediator between the mundane world and a higher state of being. If the *saṅgha* loses its power to mediate because of excessive identification with the mundane, its symbolic status will be threatened and the reciprocal bonds between the monastic order and the laity will be broken. In short, a significant reason for the existence of the monastic order will have been undermined.

B. The Changing Role of the Laity

Are Theravāda monks in Southeast Asia becoming more like their lay constituents? Perhaps, but it may be equally true that some laypersons are becoming more like monks. The ideal of Nibbāna and the practice of meditation associated with its attainment, once rather exclusively identified with the monastic vocation, has become part of the devout lay person's religious activity. Earlier we saw how U Nu encouraged Burmese civil servants to pursue the practice of meditation. Indeed, the impetus for the development of lay meditation centers in Theravāda Southeast Asia has come largely from Burma. In this section we shall look at this phenomenon. Another very important development in Theravāda countries in the modern period has been the formation of various kinds of lay Buddhist associations which have taken over, in part, some of the responsibilities formerly associated with the monastery. Sri Lanka has been especially active in this area and will provide examples of such lay organizations.

Meditation

Lay interest in meditation in Burma can be traced to a number of factors: Westerners being attracted to the practice of meditation; the revival of interest in Buddhism as part of the rise of nationalism in the late colonial period; the personal example and encouragement of the Prime Minister, U Nu; and, finally, the appearance of outstanding monastic and lay meditation teachers who developed simple methods of practice.* Three of the best known meditation masters were two monks, Ledi Sayadaw and Mahasi Sayadaw, and a layman, U Ba Khin.[112] U Nu invited Mahasi Sayadaw to come from Shwebo to Rangoon in 1949 to establish a meditation center. In December of that year the center was formally begun. Since that time branch centers have been opened elsewhere in Burma and other Theravāda countries. The Mahasi Sayadaw's methods of instruction in mindfulness (*satipaṭṭhāna vipassanā*) have been published in Burmese and several other languages including English.[113]

U Ba Khin holds a special interest, partly because he was a layman, but also because much of the *vipassanā* meditation practiced in this country is taught by Americans who studied with his students. U Ba Khin was Accountant General of the Burmese government under U Nu, and became an advocate of meditation practice out of his own personal experience. When he was about fifty years old, he developed a cancerous growth on the bone and in the flesh immediately below his right eye. In the course of some years of meditational discipline he cured himself completely. "To

**I Am A Monk* focuses on meditation and could be used to illustrate the nature of mindfulness training in the Theravāda tradition.

him the moral was obvious; a calm and pure spirit produces a healthy body and furthers efficiency in one's work."[114] To promote these goals he established the International Meditation Center in Rangoon. Winston L. King, who spent a ten-day retreat there in 1960 when U Ba Khin was still alive described the *guru-ji* as "a fascinating combination of worldly wisdom and ingeniousness, inner quiet and outward good humor, efficiency and gentleness, relaxedness and full self-control."[115]The daily schedule at the center was rigorous but not excessive, beginning with meditation at 4:30 a.m. and alternating two- and three-hour periods of meditation with one hour of rest, an hour for breakfast and for lunch, and an evening talk by U Ba Khin. King characterized the method as concentration without tension, a middle way between sloth and a sharp tight tension of mind. While many of his own personal objectives for embarking on this experience were realized, King was unable to decide whether U Ba Khin was "... a kind of genius who makes his 'system' work or whether he represents an important new type in Burmese Buddhism — the lay teacher who combines meditation and active work in a successful synthesis ...."[116] Although that particular question may be debatable, there can be no doubt that U Ba Khin, a layman, stimulated the practice of meditation as part of the daily routine of the Buddhist (and nonBuddhist) layperson.

Lay Buddhist Associations

A second important development in the changing role of the laity in Theravāda Southeast Asia has been the emergence of lay associations. In general these have promoted Buddhist education and/or social welfare. Some of them were established at the turn of the century like the Young Men's Buddhist Association of Colombo, obviously inspired by its Western counterpart. It was founded by a layman, D. D. Jayatilaka, one of the early leaders in the movement to revive Buddhism in Sri Lanka through education. He was the principal of two Buddhist colleges in Colombo, Ānanda and Dharmarājā, as well as being the general manager of the schools sponsored by the Theosophical Society. The Colombo YMBA conducts Dhamma Schools and gives Dhamma Examination aimed at providing "the youth of the land with the same standard of religious instruction and Buddhist education as was imparted by the Mahā Saṅgha in the temple schools in times before foreigners destroyed that great national institution."[117] From a beginning of 27 schools in 1919, by 1966 it had established three thousand educational centers throughout the island. Other prominent Buddhist lay organizations devoted to various kinds of education both in Sri Lanka and other countries include the Mahābodhi Society founded by the Ānagarika Dharmapāla, and the Buddhist Publication Society.[118]

Various types of lay social service organizations have arisen in Theravāda countries in the last few decades. Some of them are much like lay associations in the West affiliated with local churches. Others are national or regional in scope. In Sri Lanka several lay organizations sponsor social welfare projects. The National Council of Social Services funded under the All-Ceylon Buddhist Congress has orphanages, homes for the deaf and blind, and centers for the aged and delinquents. The Sāsana Sevaka Society, begun in 1958 with special interests in Buddhist education, also has a stated aim to help rehabilitate backward villages. The Sarvodāya Shramadāna, a rural self-help program begun about the same time, has extensive activities in 2,000 villages ranging from agriculture to health to pre-school education.[119] It has involved over 300,000 volunteers in its programs. Its founder, A. T. Ariyaratne, claims that he was inspired to found the organization by the "Lord Buddha's teaching," and interprets *sarvodāya* to mean liberation first from "the defilements within one's own mind . . . and secondly from unjust and immoral socio-economic chains."[120] He interprets the philosophy of Sarvodāya in terms of the traditional Theravāda teachings of the three characteristics of existence, dependent co-arising, the Eightfold Noble Path, and generosity (*dāna*), but gives them specifically social interpretations. For example, the Four Noble Truths are given social correlates: (1) there is a decadent village; (2) there is a cause for this decadence; (3) there is a hope that the village can reawaken; and (4) there is a way to the reawakening of all.[121]

Examples of lay Buddhist educational groups and social service foundations could be multiplied. Their proliferation underlines the ambiguity of the position of the monk. What justification remains for the monastic order if laypersons are becoming meditation teachers and performing the social services once rendered by the monastery when it was the most important organization outside of the family? Such a question is not a rhetorical one in Sri Lanka and cannot be easily ignored in either Burma or Thailand. In Cambodia and Laos revolutionary forces saw the *saṅgha* either as reactionary or as a hindrance to political and economic development. If similar revolutionary forces gain prominence in Sri Lanka, Burma, and Thailand, the fate of the Theravāda monastic order may hang in the balance. Whether the monk can continue to symbolize values of lasting significance embodied in the ideals of Buddhism and at the same time speak to the needs of societies in radical transition is a fundamental issue not merely for the academic study of Buddhism and Society in Southeast Asia but the very survival of this religious tradition as we have known it.

Can Theravāda Buddhism which has been such an integral part of the societies of Sri Lanka, Burma, Thailand, Laos and Cambodia maintain itself in a form resembling the description in the preceding chapters? To be sure the past few years have brought drastic changes to much of that part of the world, so drastic that the Buddhist worldview and the institutions which have fostered it are seriously endangered. In Cambodia and Laos the Buddhist *saṅgha* has been disestablished. The sacred monarchial traditions of Southeast Asia, largely undermined during the colonial period, exist only in vague, vestigial forms. The old religious festivals which once shaped community life are losing their meaning. A smaller percentage of the male population is being ordained into the Buddhist monkhood. Nevertheless, in much of rural Southeast Asia the traditional rites, rituals and festivals still bind people together in a common identity, Buddhist values still play a normative role in a peoples' view of social wellbeing and personal salvation, and Buddhist institutions have made some creative adjustments to economic, social and political changes. In short, the effort we have made to understand Buddhism and society in Southeast Asia with the aid of audio-visual resources has a contemporary as well as a historical relevance. Whether looking at the past or present our emphasis has been on the problem of meaning and cross-cultural interpretation, and it is for the reasons of more complete understanding and more adequate cultural interpretation that we have argued for the use of films and other audio-visual aids along with the descriptive and analytical apparatus of this essay.

Notes

1. Wilfred Cantwell Smith, "The Study of Religion and the Study of the Bible," *Journal of the American Academy of Religion* XXIX:2 (June, 1971), pp. 131-140.

2. A good example of this point would be the film, *The Temple of the Twenty Pagodas*. Its minimal sound track enhances the visual impact of the temple activities being seen by the viewer. In the hands of a skillful and knowledgeable teacher, the discussion of the film elaborates and clarifies conceptually what has been seen but without detracting from the admittedly vaguer, yet possibly more profound level of understanding gained through the film.

3. See Donald K. Swearer, *Secrets of the Lotus* (New York: Macmillan & Co., 1971).

4. See Robert N. Bellah, "Religious Revolution," in *Beyond Belief* (New York: Harper & Row, 1970).

5. Here I am alluding to G. Van Der Leeuw's classic study, *Religion in Essence and Manifestation* (New York: Harper & Row, 1963).

6. *Ethos* and *worldview* are being used here in the sense defined by Clifford Geertz in his article, "Ethos, World View, and the Analysis of Sacred Symbols," in Clifford Geertz, *The Interpretation of Cultures* (New York: Basic Books, Inc., 1973), p. 127: "A people's ethos is the tone, character and quality of their life, its moral and aesthetic style and mood; it is the underlying attitude toward themselves and their world that life reflects. Their world view is their picture of the way things in sheer actuality are, their concept of nature, of self, of society. It contains their most comprehensive ideas of order."

7. In most cases Buddhist terms will be in their Pāli form, the scriptural language of Theravāda Buddhism. When the context demands, the Sanskrit or a vernacular term will be used.

8. See Max Weber, *The Religion of India*, trans. and ed. by Hans H. Gerth and Don Martindale (New York: The Free Press, 1958), chaps. 6 and 7.

9. Melford E. Spiro, *Buddhism & Society. A Great Tradition and Its Burmese Vicissitudes* (New York: Harper & Row, 1970).

10. Winston L. King, *In the Hope of Nibbana. An Essay on Theravada Buddhist Ethics* (LaSalle: Open Court, 1964).

11. The Jātakas purport to be stories of previous lives of the Buddha. Since they are folk traditions incorporated into a set form and tied together by the *bodhisattva* concept, they provide a rich source for the popular tradition of Indian Buddhism.

12. Margaret Cone and Richard Gombrich, *The Perfect Generosity of Prince Vessantara* (Oxford: The Clarendon Press, 1977).

13. Spiro, *op. cit.*, p. 192.

14. *Ibid.*

15. See Michael Ames, "Magical-Animism and Buddhism: A Structural Analysis of the Sinhalese Religious System," *The Journal of Asian Studies*, XXIII (June, 1964), pp. 21-52.

16. Gananath Obeyesekere, "The Buddhist Pantheon in Ceylon and Its Extensions," *Anthropological Studies in Theravada Buddhism*, ed. by M. Nash (New Haven: Yale University Southeast Asian Studies, 1966), pp. 1-27.

17. See Spiro, *op. cit.*

18. See S. J. Tambiah, *Buddhism and Spirit Cults in Northeast Thailand*, Cambridge Studies in Social Anthropology, vol. 2 (London: Cambridge University Press, 1970).

19. See Spiro, *op. cit.*, p. 227.

20. See Tambiah, *op. cit.*, p. 158.

21. Spiro, *op. cit.*, p. 301.

22. Richard F. Gombrich, "Consecration of a Buddha Image," *Journal of Asian Studies*, XXVI:1, (1966), pp. 23-36.

23. A. K. Coomaraswamy, *Medieval Sinhalese Art*, 2nd ed. (New York: Pantheon Books, 1956), p. 71.

24. Tambiah, *op. cit.*, p. 153.

25. Donald K. Swearer, *Wat Haripūñjaya. A Study of the Royal Temple of the Buddha's Relic, Lamphun, Thailand*, AAR Studies in Religion No. 10 (Missoula: Scholars Press, 1976), pp. 43-46.

26. Swearer, *op. cit.*, ch. 3.

27. Phya Anuman Rajadhon, *Essays on Thai Folklore* (Bangkok: Social Science Association Press, 1968), p. 39.

28. Kenneth E. Wells, *Thai Buddhism. Its Rites and Activities* (Bangkok: Suriyabun Publishers, 1975), p. 114.

29. Singkha Wannasai, *Praphaeni Lae Ngan Nakkhatriksa Haeng Lānnā Thai.* [Customs and Astrological Celebrations of Lanna Thai]. Mimeograph, n.d., p. 1. Taken from the Northern Thai Chronicle, *Cāmādevīvaṁsa.*

30. Phya Anuman, *op. cit.*, p. 39.

31. Tambiah, *op. cit.*, p. 192.

32. Sukumar Dutt. *Buddhist Monks and Monasteries of India.*

33. See the *bhikkhu vagga* chapter of the *Dhammapāda.*

34. Spiro, *op. cit.*, p. 322.

35. *Ibid.*, p. 338.

36. Donald K.Swearer, "The Layman Extraordinaire in Northern Thai Buddhism," *Journal of the Siam Society* 64:1 (Jan. 1976), pp. 151-168.

37. Wells, *op. cit.*, p. 142.

38. For example see Shway Yoe, *The Burman. His Life and Notions* (W. W. Norton & Co., 1963), chap. 64; S. J. Tambiah, *op. cit.*, chap. 11.

39. I am particularly indebted to Konrad Kingshall, *Ku Daeng. The Red Tomb. A Village Study in Northern Thailand*, 3rd ed. (Bangkok: Suriyaban, 1976), pp. 206-224.

40. Wells, *op. cit.*, pp. 214-215.

41. Kingshill, *op. cit.*, p. 212.

42. Tambiah, *op. cit.*, p. 180; Kingshill, *op. cit.*, p. 212.

43. Kingshill, *op. cit.*, pp. 220-223.

44. Bardwell L. Smith, ed., *Religion and Legitimation of Power in Sri Lanka*, (Chambersburg: Anima Books, 1978); Bardwell L. Smith, ed., *Religion and Legitimation of Power in Thailand, Laos, and Burma* (Chambersburg: Anima Books, 1978); Manuel Sarkisyanz, *Buddhist Backgrounds of the Burmese Revolution* (The Hague: Martinus Nijhoff, 1965); S. J. Tambiah, *World Conqueror and World Renouncer. A Study of Buddhism and Polity in Thailand Against A Historical Background*, Cambridge Studies in Social Anthropology, 15 (London: Cambridge University Press, 1976).

45. *The Glass Palace Chronicle of the Kings of Burma*, trans. by Pe Maung Tin and G. H. Luce (London: Oxford University Press, 1923), pp. 6-7.

46. *Ibid.*, p. xiii.

47. Ratanapañña Thera, *The Sheaf of Garlands of the Epochs of the Conqueror (Jinakālamālīpakaraṇam)*, trans. by N. A. Jayawickrama. Pali Text Society Translation Series, 36

(London: Luzac & Co., 1968), pp. 107-108.

48. *Ibid.*, p. 109.

49. See Frank E. Reynolds' fascinating article, "The Holy Emerald Jewel: Some Aspects of Buddhist Symbolism and Political Legitimation in Thailand and Laos," in Bardwell L. Smith, ed. *Religion and Legitimation of Power in Thailand, Laos, and Burma*, pp. 173-193.

50. Adapted from Frank E. Reynolds, *op. cit.*, p. 176.

51. *Ibid.*, pp. 183-184.

52. See S. J. Tambiah, *World Conqueror and World Renouncer*, chap. 2.

53. Hermann Kulke, *The Devarājā.* Southeast Asia Program Data Paper 108 (Ithaca: Cornell University, 1978). Kulke challenges the standard interpretation of the *devarājā* notion.

54. George Coedès, *Angkor. An Introduction* (London: Oxford University Press, 1966), p. 31.

55. Robert Heine-Geldern, *Conceptions of State and Kingship in Southeast Asia.* Southeast Asia Program Data Paper 18 (Ithaca: Cornell University, 1958), pp. 5-6.

56. See J. Filliozat, "New Researches on the Relations Between India and Cambodia," *Indica* (Bombay), III, pp. 95-106; I. W. Mabbett, "Devaraja," *Journal of Southeast Asian History*, X, pp. 202ff; Kulke, *op. cit.*

57. H. Kulke, *op. cit.*, p. 3.

58. See H. G. Quartich Wales, *The Making of Greater India* (London: Bernard Quartich, 1961); George Coedès, *The Indianized States of Southeast Asia*, ed. W. F. Vella (Honolulu: University of Hawaii Press, 1968); Heinrich Zimmer, *The Art of Indian Asia*, 2nd ed., vol. 1. Bollingen Series XXXIX (New York: Pantheon Books, 1960), pp. 298-317; A. K. Coomaraswamy, *History of Indian and Indonesian Art* (New York: Dover Publications, 1965), pp. 203-216.

59. Reginald le May, *The Culture of Southeast Asia* (London: George Allen & Unwin Ltd., 1954), p. 98.

60. Heinrich Zimmer, *op. cit.*, p. 301. Quoted from N. J. Krom, *The Life of the Buddha on the Stupa of Barabudur According to the Lalitavistara Text*, 1926.

61. Paul Mus, *Barabadur: Esquisse d'une histoire du Bouddhisme foundée la critique archéologique des textes.* (Hanoi: École Française d'Extreme-Orient, 1932).

62. H. G. Quartich Wales, *op. cit.*, p. 123, referring to J. C. de Casparis, *Prasasti Indonesia*, I, 1950.

63. Quartich Wales, *op. cit.*, p. 124.

64. A. K. Coomaraswamy, *op. cit.*, p. 204.

65. George Coedès, *The Making of Southeast Asia*, trans. by H. M. Wright (Berkeley: University of California Press, 1966), p. 57.

66. Lawrence P. Briggs, "The Syncretism of Religions in Southeast Asia, Especially in the Khmer Empire," *Journal of the American Oriental Society*, 71:4 (1950), p. 235.

67. H. G. Quartich Wales, *The Making of Greater India*, p. 188.

68. *Ibid.*, p. 195.

69. Heinrich Zimmer, *op. cit.*, p. 210.

70. See A. K. Coomaraswamy, *op. cit.*, pp. 192-194; Heinrich Zimmer, *op. cit.*, pp. 209-212; Bernard Groslier & Jacques Arthaud, *Angkor. Art & Civilization*, rev. ed. (New York: Frederick A. Praeger, 1966).

71. See G. Coedès, *Angkor. An Introduction*, chap. 5.

72. H. Zimmer, *op. cit.*, p. 211. See also Aung Thaw, *Historical Sites in Burma* (Rangoon: Ministry of Culture, 1972), chap. 5; Reginald Le May, *op. cit.*, chap. 3.

73. Aung Thaw, *op. cit.*, p. 58.

74. Alexander B. Griswold, et. al., *The Art of Burma, Korea, Tibet* (New York: Crown Publishers, Inc., 1964), p. 36.

75. Charles F. Keyes, *The Golden Peninsula. Culture and Adaptation in Mainland Southeast Asia*

(New York: Macmillan Publishing Co., 1977), p. 72.

76. Pillar Edict, No. 2. Quoted in T. W. Rhys Davids, *Buddhist India*, 8th ed. (Calcutta: Susil Gupta, 1959), p. 134.

77. See S. J. Tambiah's fascinating analysis in *World Conqueror and World Renouncer*, chap. 2.

78. Bardwell L. Smith, "The Ideal Social Order as Portrayed in the Chronicles of Ceylon," in *The Two Wheels of Dhamma. Essays on the Theravada Tradition in India and Ceylon*, ed., B. L. Smith. AAR Studies in Religion, No. 3 (Chambersburg: American Academy of Religion, 1972), p. 40. In the same volume see, Frank E. Reynolds, "The Two Wheels of Dhamma: A Study of Early Buddhism."

79. Sukumar Dutt, *The Buddha and Five After-Centuries* (London: Luzac & Co., 1957), p. 174.

80. *Ibid.*, p. 168.

81. H. Zimmer, *op. cit.*, p. 233.

82. S. Dutt, *op. cit.*, p. 178.

83. H. Zimmer, *op. cit.*, p. 236.

84. *Ibid.*, p. 233.

85. S. Dutt, *op. cit.*, p. 170.

86. Government of the Union of Burma Land Nationalization Act, 1948, p. 29, para 9, quoted in Manuel Sarkisyanz, *Buddhist Backgrounds of the Burmese Revolution*, p. 215.

87. See D. K. Swearer, *Buddhism in Transition* (Philadelphia: Westminster Press, 1970), pp. 38ff.

88. *The Nation*, October 1958, quoted in Richard Butwell, *U Nu of Burma* (Palo Alto: Stanford University Press, 1963), p. 62.

89. Donald E. Smith, *Religion & Politics in Burma* (Princeton: Princeton University Press, 1965), pp. 318-319.

90. Heinz Bechert, "S. W. R. D. Bandaranaike and the Legitimation of Power through Buddhist Ideals," in Bardwell L. Smith (ed.), *Religion and Legitimation of Power in Sri Lanka*, p. 204.

91. S. W. R. D. Bandaranaike, *Speeches and Writings* (Colombo: Dept. of Broadcasting and Information, 1963), p. 308.

92. For a discussion of contemporary trends in Theravāda Buddhism in Southeast Asian countries see Heinrich Dumoulin and John C. Maraldo (eds.), *The Cultural Political & Religious Significance of Buddhism in the Modern World* (New York: Collier Books, 1976).

93. Thich Nhat Hahn, *Lotus in a Sea of Fire* (London: SCM Press Ltd., 1961).

94. For a popular and somewhat unbalanced treatment of this issue see Jerrold Schechter, *The New Face of Buddha* (Tokyo: John Weatherhill, Inc., 1967).

95. *The Buddhist* XXXVIII/2 (July, 1967), p. 47.

96. For a study of Bhikkhu Kitthivuḍḍho see Charles F. Keyes, "Political Crisis and Militant Buddhism in Contemporary Thailand," in Bardwell L. Smith, *Religion and Legitimation of Power in Thailand, Laos and Burma*. I have written extensively on Bhikkhu Buddhadāsa, most recently, "Bhikkhu Buddhadāsa on Ethics and Society," *Journal of Religious Ethics* 7:1 (1979), pp. 54-64.

97. Kitthivuddho, *Sing Thī Kuan Kham Nu'ng* (Bangkok: Abhidhamma Foundation, 1971), p. 8.

98. *Ibid.*, p. 24.

99. Charles F. Keyes, "Political Crisis and Militant Buddhism in Contemporary Thailand," p. 153.

100. *Ibid.*

101. Kitthivuḍḍho, *Khā Communist Māi Pāpa* [Killing Communists is not Demeritorious]. (Bangkok: Abhidhamma Foundation, 1976), pp. 49-52.

102. *Ibid.*, p. 48.

103. Some of these have been collected in *Toward the Truth*, ed. by Donald K. Swearer (Philadelphia: Westminster, 1970).

104. Interview. November 10, 1976.

105. Buddhadāsa, *Kan Tham Ngan Duai Citta Wāng [Working With a Liberated Mind] (Bangkok: Society for the Propagation of Buddhism, 1975), p. 13.*

106. Ibid., pp. 14-15.

107. F. Bruce Morgan, "Vocation of Monk and Layman: Signs of Change in Thai Buddhist Ethics," in *Tradition & Change in Theravada Buddhism.* Contributions to Asian Studies, vol. 4, ed. Bardwell L. Smith (Leiden: E. J. Brill, 1973), p. 71.

108. E. Michael Mendelson, *Sangha and State in Burma. A Study of Monastic Sectarianism and Leadership*, ed. by John P. Ferguson (Ithaca: Cornell University Press, 1975), pp. 306ff.

109. Donald K. Swearer, *Buddhism in Transition*, pp. 46ff.

110. Phra Maha Chai Aphakaro, "Kan Praprung Botbat Khong Phra Sangha," [Reforming the Role of the Sangha], *Kalpa Phrksa* 1:1 (1972), p. 1.

111. *Ibid.*, see pp. 14-23.

112. See Winston L. King, "Contemporary Burmese Buddhism," in *Buddhism in the Modern World*, ed. by Heinrich Dumoulin and John C. Maraldo, pp. 95-96.

113. Mahasi Sayadaw, *The Progress of Insight* (Kandy: Forest Hermitage, 1965); *Practical Insight Meditation.* (Kandy: Forest Hermitage, 1971).

114. Winston L. King, *A Thousand Lives Away* (Cambridge: Harvard University Press, 1974), p. 227.

115. *Ibid.*, pp. 226-227.

116. *Ibid.*, p. 227.

117. *The Buddhist.* XXXVII/1 (June 1966), p. 7.

118. See Donald K. Swearer, "Lay Buddhism and the Buddhist Revival in Ceylon," *Journal of the American Academy of Religion* XXXVIII: 3 (Sept. 1970), pp. 266ff.

119. Joanna Rogers Macy, "Dependent Co-Arising: The Distinctiveness of Buddhist Ethics," *Journal of Religious Ethics*, 7:1 (Spring 1979), p. 49.

120. *Ibid.*, p. 49.

121. *Ibid.*, p. 50.

APPENDIX
I

Audio-Visual Resources

As the audio-visual references throughout the body of the essay indicate, films and other types of audio-visual aids relevant to the teaching of Buddhism and society in Southeast Asia vary greatly in quality and scope of subject matter. Some of the older, more widely known and used films such as *Theravada Buddhism* (17 minutes) in the Altars of the World series produced by Lew Ayers and reissued in 1975 are only marginally acceptable for classroom use. This particular film, for example, surveys the life of the Buddha, his teachings, the monastic community, and various Theravāda practices. It suffers from oversimplification and a lack of clear cultural context. The film's inaccuracies include the claim that Theravāda monks are always vegetarians, discusses Buddhist doctrine to the irrelevant visual background of a Burmese ear-piercing ceremony, and makes misleading comparisons between Theravāda and Mahāyāṇa Buddhism in the brief study guide. *The Buddhist World* (11 minutes, Coronet Instructional Films) suffers from excessive simplicity, generalities, stereotypes and cliches, but is listed as being available for rental from at least 14 university film libraries. Such films should be replaced by newer, more doctrinally accurate and culturally illuminating films which will be discussed below.

Other films and slide sets have a specific focus and can be articulated into a course design to meet specific needs. For example, a class period on the Buddha might use slides from *The Evolution of the Buddha Image* (The Asia Society) or *The Story of the Buddha in Thai Murals* (New York University Asian Studies Curriculum Center). Films on this topic have a variety of shortcomings but the following could be used as part of a classroom presentation (See *Focus on Buddhism* for descriptions and evaluations of these materials.): *Thai Images of the Buddha* (Indiana University), *The Buddha: Temple Complex at Borobudur* (Radim Films), *Gautama the Buddha* (Information Services of India), or *Awareness* (Mass Media Ministries). Other specific topics for which audio-visual materials exist include mediation (e.g., *I Am A Monk* Hartley Productions), ordination ceremony (e.g., the slide set, *Monk's Ordination Ceremony* — New York University Asian Studies Curriculum Center), Buddhist archaeological sites (e.g., *Immortal Stupa* — Information Services of India), classical Hindu-Buddhist centers (e.g., *Angkor: The Lost City* — Pennsylvania State University), and films which are more generally cultural but include aspects of Theravāda Buddhism (e.g., *Chiang Mai, Northern Capital* — Australian Information Service).

Of the films on Theravāda Buddhism in the three major Theravāda cultures today three stand out: *Buddhism: Footprint of the Buddha* (Sri Lanka), *Vejen* (Burma), and *Buddhism: Be Ye Lamps Unto Yourselves* (Thailand). Three additional films are also of superior quality: *Smile* (Burma), *Temple of the Twenty Pagodas* (Thailand), and *Buddhism: The Path to Nirvana* (Sri Lanka). The slide set, *Buddhism in Southeast Asia and Ceylon*, and the film strip, *The Buddhist Tradition: Buddhism in Burma* make a valuable contribution to the stock of available, noteworthy instructional visuals. The remainder of this discussion will focus on each of these individual resources.

Buddhism: Footprint of the Buddha (54 minutes) is one of thirteen films in the popular series, The Long Search, produced by the BBC and shown on Public Broadcast Television networks in this country. The film takes the viewer on a trip to Sri Lanka to search for the nature of Theravada Buddhism as it is lived, practiced and taught. We see Sri Lankan Buddhism through the eyes of Ronald Eyre, the observer-interlocuter, who begins his search at the impressive rock-cut statues of the Buddha at Polonnaruwa, and then moves sequentially to the site of the Buddha's enlightenment at Bodhgaya in India, an ordination ceremony, monks on their morning food-rounds (*piṇḍapata*), a rains-retreat (*vassa*) ceremony on the May full-moon sabbath day, and finally to monks meditating at the Dambulla cave monastery north of Kandy, the last seat of the Sinhalese monarchy. These stops provide occasions for a discussion of Theravāda beliefs and practices including the moral precepts and the Eightfold Noble Path, the nature of the Buddha, astrology, supernatural powers, gift-giving and merit, and the nature of Buddhist mindfulness. The film is structured around the poles of withdrawal/meditation and involvement/service both of which are part of the Buddhist's journey to a higher goal (Nibbāna) achieved by one's own effort without reliance on an outside power or authority.

The comprehensiveness of this film makes it ideal as the basis of a study of the interrelationships between the normative and contextual aspects of Theravāda Buddhism. Although sometimes we find Eyre's questions overemphasize certain issues, e.g., salvation is not achieved by faith in an outside power, the presence of the interlocuter serves to provoke a questioning mood on the part of the viewer. The richness of the film makes it appropriate for two showings followed by discussion or as the basis of a response paper which would be revised after further study and the second showing.

Vejen, (22 minutes) directed by Per Holst and distributed through Carousel Films, attempts to have us act as a participant in Burmese Buddhism rather than as an observer. The film focuses on the activities of a young boy who attends to the needs of a senior monk. We see ritual activities at the Shwe Dagon Pagoda in Rangoon, an informal class at a monastery, monks on their food rounds, and finally, the boy's ordination as a novice (*shin-byu*). Against this background the narration discusses some of the essential teachings and ideals of the Theravāda tradition, e.g.,*kamma, saṁsāra*, Nibbāna. The film conveys simplicity and directness without sacrificing the essentially human or rich variety of Burmese Buddhism. The sequence on the *shin-byu* ceremony could become a part of a discussion of the ordination ritual in which films, such as the following, were used.

Buddhism: Be Ye Lamps Unto Yourselves (29 minutes) directed by Howard Enders for the ABC *Directions* program was filmed in Bangkok and environs. Structured around two ordination ceremonies, it also includes scenes of a variety of monastic activities including meditation and study. Its sequence on morning food rounds (*piṇḍapata*), an activity which seems to make its way into most of the recent films on Theravāda Buddhism in Southeast Asia, has some exceptinally beautiful photography. It is also the only major film to include a funeral ceremony. The narration not only explains the visual background but discusses the cardinal teachings of Thai Buddhism through interviews and quotations from Theravāda texts.

Cinematographically all three of these films are exceptional as are the three discussed below. *Footprint of the Buddha, Vejen*, and *Be Ye Lamps Unto Yourselves* are generally better, however, in terms of the range of the teachings and practices presented and the quality of the narrative interpretation.

Of all the recommended films on Southeast Asian Buddhism *The Smile* (20 minutes) most subtly raises the question about the nature of Buddhism within a particular cultural context. Produced by Serge Bourguignon and available through several university film rental libraries, *The Smile* is a reenactment of a day in the life of a young Burmese novice who attends an elderly monk. The polarity is drawn between the old man who seems to symbolize the meditative attainments of equanimity and non-attachment, and the young boy who obviously enjoys life as he encounters it: a water buffalo in the field, a leaf worm's handiwork, Burmese boxers, lovely girls bathing at a well, and a traveling puppet show. The film raises the question of the paradox between the Nibbanic ideal and the actual experience of Buddhism within a particular culture. It can be used effectively to discuss the two faces of Buddhism not as oppositional but as they interact and compliment one another. What is Buddhism? The elderly monk who seems somewhat removed from the world? Or the young boy who smiles at the water buffalo? Or is it both?

In contrast to the above films *Temple of the Twenty Pagodas* (20 minutes) directed by Brian Haunant for the Australian Information Services focuses on a particular Thai *wat* (temple-monastery), the activities of the monks there, and the interaction between monks and laity. It includes scenes of monks chanting, on their food rounds, cleaning the temple precincts, studying, eating a noon meal, and speaking to lay visitors. The camera takes us outside of the monastery compound to farmers in nearby rice fields and follows school children playing inside the compound in an attempt to illustrate the fluid boundaries of the Thai *wat*. Unfortunately the film is marred by lack of narration so the uninformed viewer will not be aware of the significance of the amulets being purchased by the lay visitors, the meaning of monks prostrating before the image of the Buddha, or of one of the monks talking with a group of civil servants. If the instructor has sufficient background to interpret these scenes, however, the lack of narrative explanation can make the film even more useful as the basis of a class discussion.

The least effective of these six films but still useful and of a high quality is *Buddhism: The Path to Enlightenment* (30 minutes) produced by Hartley Films. The beautiful photography includes scenes from Buddhist pilgrimage sites in India but focuses on various religious activities in Sri Lanka including offerings before Buddha images, walking meditation, monks receiving food from laypersons, circumambulating *stūpas*, and the Kandy procession (*perahara*) during the month of *asalah* (July or August) led by the famous Temple of the Tooth. Unfortunately the narration is rather superficial and oversimplified in comparison with the films mentioned above.

Although the pioneering set of slides on Buddhism by Kenneth Morgan (*Buddhism*, Visual Education Service, Yale Divinity School) contains pictures of important Theravāda historical sites, it is of less general value than the newer *Buddhism in Southeast Asia and Ceylon* and *The Buddhist Tradition: Buddhism in Burma* which are more focused on Southeast Asia. The former was produced by Charles Kennedy as part of the Asian Religions Media Resources and comes with a

36-page guide. While the slides and their descriptions are of an uneven quality, they cover the major Buddhist countries in Southeast Asia (Burma, 1-45, Sri Lanka, 46-95, Thailand, 96-157, Laos, 158-164, Cambodia, 165-186, and also Indonesia, 180-220). Included in the set are festivals, temple and home rituals, meditation, famous Buddhist monuments, a funeral ceremony, and a few of the contemporary developments within the Theravāda *saṅghas*.

The Buddhist Tradition: Buddhism in Burma which is part of the Argus Communications' Religion in Human Culture series focuses almost exclusively on Burma but is supplemented by pictures from Sri Lanka and Thailand to accommodate the narration provided by a filmstrip guide and a cassette tape. Scenes relate to both lay and monastic religious practice and depict the nature and goals of the monastic life, the role of nuns, the relationships between monks and laypersons, a novitiate ordination, pagoda rites, and the relationship between Buddhism and the *nat* spirit cult. Although the guide is on a fairly general level, the interpretative comments are helpful as well as the discussion questions and follow-up activities.

Even though films have the advantage of involving the viewer in a dynamic sequence of events, slides can sometimes be integrated more easily into a particular lecture format. For purposes of classroom discussion a short film followed by slides focusing on particular practices or activities can be particularly effective. Unfortunately, such a set of audio-visual resources is not readily available for Buddhism as it is for the Hindu rites of passage filmed by Daniel Smith of Syracuse University.

APPENDIX II

Bibliography

1. George Coedès, *The Indianized States of Southeast Asia*, ed. W. F. Vella. Honolulu: University of Hawaiaa Press, 1978. Although Coedès tends to give his interpretations of classical Southeast Asian culture a Khmer slant, his work stands as a benchmark for cultural historians. His *The Making of Southeast Asia* (Berkeley, 1964) lacks the detail of his larger cultural history and focuses exclusively on mainland Southeast Asia.
2. Clifford Geertz, *The Interpretation of Cultures*. New York: Basic Books, Inc., 1973. Geertz's work on Java and Islamic cultures are seminal studies and his theoretical contribution to cultural anthropology ranks with the very best.
3. Richard F. Gombrich, *Precept and Practice. Traditional Buddhism in the Rural Highlands of Ceylon*. Oxford: Clarendon Press, 1971. Gombrich brings to this synchronic study the training of a philologist and the eye of a historian.
4. Robert Heine-Geldern, *Conceptions of State and Kingship in Southeast Asia.* Southeast Asia Program Data Paper No. 18. Ithaca: Cornell University, 1958. Heine-Geldern's paper on religion and kingship in Southeast Asia has had a pervasive influence only recently seriously challenged by scholars like Hermann Kulke (*The Devarājā*, Southeast Asia Program Data Paper No. 108. Ithaca: Cornell University, 1978).
5. Charles F. Keyes, *The Golden Peninsula, Culture and Adaptationin Mainland Southeast Asia.* New York: Macmillan Publishing Co., 1977. The best recent study of the cultures of mainland Southeast Asia.
6. Winston L. King, *A Thousand Lives Away.* Cambridge: Harvard University Press, 1974. A study of contemporary Theravāda Buddhism in Burma with helpful chapters on Theravāda cosmology, the interrelationship between popular and normative levels of Buddhism, and the reaction of Burmese Buddhism to modern science.
7. Robert C. Lester, *Theravada Buddhism in Southeast Asia.* Ann Arbor: University of Michigan Press, 1973. A clearly written, comprehensive look at Theravāda Buddhism against the historical, cultural and contemporary background of Southeast Asia.
8. Manning Nash et. al., *Anthropological Studies in Theravada Buddhism.* Southeast Asia Studies Cultural Report Series No. 13. New Haven: Yale University, 1966. Although this volume is now fifteen years old it contains some of the most useful articles on Theravāda Buddhism written by anthropologists working in Theravāda cultures.
9. Bardwell L. Smith, ed., *Religion and Legitimation of Power in Sri Lanka.* Chambersburg: Anima Books, 1978. This volume and its companion, *Religion and Legitimation of Power in Thailand, Laos and Burma.* Chambersburg: Anima

Books, 1978, make a major contribution to a field in which there was extensive study in the early 60s.

10. Melford E. Spiro, *Buddhism & Society. A Great Tradition and Its Burmese Vicissitudes.* New York: Harper & Row, 1970. Spiro's sometimes controversial interpretations do not take away from the value of the tremendous amount of information contained in this volume.

11. Donald K. Swearer, *Buddhism in Tradition.* Philadelphia: Westminster Press, 1969. A brief survey of some of the major trends in contemporary Buddhism in Southeast Asia.

12. ________________, *Wat Haripuñjaya. A Study of the Royal Temple of the Buddha's Relic, Lamphun, Thailand.* AAR Studies in Religion No. 10. Missoula: Scholars Press, 1976. A diachronic and synchronic study of one of the major religious centers in northern Thailand.

13. S. J. Tambiah, *Buddhism and Spirit Cults in Northeast Thailand.* Cambridge Studies in Social Anthropology, vol. 2. London: Cambridge University Press, 1970. Tambiah's study of Theravāda Buddhism within a northeastern village context still stands as the most useful work on Thai Buddhism.

14. ________________, *World Conqueror & World Renouncer. A Study of Buddhism and Polity in Thailand Against a Historical Background.* Cambridge Studies in Social Anthropology, vol. 15. London: Cambridge University Press, 1976. Although somewhat turgidly written and more structuralist than his earlier study, Tambiah's interpretation of the "galactic" polity of classical Thai culture and the information he provides on the contemporary *saṅgha* make this study an important one.

15. Heinrich Zimmer, *The Art of Indian Asia*, 2 vols. Bollingen Series. New York: Pantheon Books, 1960. In most courses on Buddhism insufficient attention is given to art. There are excellent studies of the great monuments such as Borobudur and Angkor and more general surveys of the art of Southeast Asia (e.g. Philip Rawson). Still, Zimmer's study of Indian art is a must for any historian of religion interested in Buddhism.

APPENDIX III

Glossary

Abhidhamma	Literally the "higher (*abhi*) teaching (*dhamma*)." Refers to the third division (*piṭaka*) of the Pāli language scriptures of Theravāda Buddhism. Contains a diverse body of texts but many of them represent more technical or scholastic interpretations of the dialogue (*sutta*) texts.
Ādi Buddha	Literally the beginning or original Buddha. In Mahāyāṇa and Vajrayāṇa Buddhism often identified as the central Buddha of the five *dhyani* Buddhas; usually the Buddha Vairocana.
Ānanda	In the Pāli *suttas* texts of Theravāda Buddhism Ānanda appears as one of the most important disciples of the Buddha. From a literary point of view Ānanda acts as a foil to the Buddha in the famous *Mahā-parinibbāna Sutta*.
Anawratā	(1040-1077 A.D.). Considered to be the founder of the unified Burmese kingdom with the capital at Pagan.
Aggañña Suttanta	One of the *suttas* in the Long Discourses (*Dīgha Nikāya*) which deals with the origin of the world and the reason for the selection of a righteous ruler.
Anattā	Literally "not (*an-*) self (*attā*)." One of the seminal concepts in the teachings of the Buddha. Often misinterpreted as a world-denying term.
Āsālahā Pūjā	A celebration remembering the Buddha's first discourse, "Setting the Wheel of the Law in Motion" (*Dhammacakkappavattana Sutta*) delivered at the Deer Park in Vārāṇasī. It occurs in the full moon sabbath of the eighth lunar month (*āsālahā*).
Bhikkhu	The term used to designate monastic followers of the Buddha. Literally, "beggar," the word refers to the fact that Theravāda monks depend upon the generosity of the laity for their material well-being. The Theravāda monastic order is referred to as the *bhikkhu-saṅgha*.
Bodhisattva	Literally, a "wisdom (*bodhi*) being (*sattva*)." In the Theravāda tradition the term refers to the Buddha in his various earthly forms. In the Mahāyāṇa tradition the term comes to be applied to all beings seeking enlightenment, or those who will be future Buddhas.
Brahmaloka	Literally, the "world (*loka*) of Brahma," one of the abodes of the gods in the Theravāda cosmology.
Cakkavatti	Literally, a "wheel-turner." The term refers to the Buddhist monarch whose power in the secular realm parallels the power of the Buddha in the sacred realm.

Cakkavatti Sīhanāda Suttanta — A *sutta* in the Long Discourses (*Dīgha Nikāya* which is an important source of information about the traditional understanding of the *cakkavatti* concept.

Cao — A Thai term with several different possible meanings: spirit, deity, lord.

Cetiya — A mound or sepulchral monument. A reliquary containing remains of the Buddha, saints (*arahant*) or highly revered Buddhist leaders. In Thai the term is transformed into *cedi*.

Chiang Mai — The most important city in northern Thailand. The dominant power among various principalities in northern Thailand from the end of the thirteenth century.

Dāna — The virtue of generosity, one of the principal Theravāda moral perfections (*pāramitā*).

Devarājā — Literally, "god-king." Thought to have been a notion of divine kingship which developed in the Khmer kingdom in the ninth century and which played an important role in the monarchial traditions of the classical states of Southeast Asia.

Dhamma — A basic concept in Theravāda thought. It can mean the basic constituents of reality, the truth, the teachings of the Buddha. The Buddha's first discourse is entitled, "Setting the Wheel of the Truth (or Law) in Motion," (*Dhammacakkapavattana Sutta*).

Dhātu-garbha — The Pāli form of the Sinhalese term, *dāgoba*, referring to a mound reliquary, i.e., a *cetiya*.

Dhyāni Buddha — Literally, "meditation Buddha." In Vajrayāṇa Buddhism the five Buddhas of the center and four cardinal directions, e.g. the Buddha Amitābha of the West.

Dīpavaṃsa — The *Island Chronicle*, one of the three major chronicles of Sinhalese Buddhism.

Divyāvadāna — A Mahāyāṇa Buddhist text which contains one of the most famous legendary accounts of the life of the Buddha.

Duṭṭhagāmaṇi (101-77 B.C.) — Ruler of Sri Lanka who is famous for defeating the Tamils and reuniting the country under Sinhalese rule.

Gaṇḍavyūha — A Mahāyāṇa text concerned with the enlightenment quest of Sudhana. Sometimes referred to as a Mahāyāṇa "Pilgrim's Progress."

Haripuñjaya — The pre-Thai center of culture and political power in northern Thailand. It was defeated by the Thais in the thirteenth century. Now known as Lamphun.

Indra — A Hindu deity of greatest importance in Vedic times. In Buddhism Indra is known as *Sakka*, the ruler of the gods.

Jātaka — The Pāli canon has 547 *jātaka* stories, tales based on folk legends which have been made into episodes purporting to be previous lives of the Buddha.

Jātakamālā — A "Garland of Birth Stories." A Sanskrit rendering of 34 *jātakas* ascribed to Ārya Sūra who may have lived in the first century A.D.

Kamma (Sanskrit *karma*) Together with *dhamma* the most important term in Theravada Buddhist thought. In general parlance it means act or action; however, technically it refers tothe Law of Kamma, i.e., that good acts will bring good consequences and vice versa.

Kapilavastu An important city in northern India during the lifetime of the Buddha.

Karuṇā The moral perfection of compassion.

Kaṭhina The robes presented to Buddhist monks at the end of the three-month rains retreat period of confinement. The *kaṭhina* usually takes place during the month of November.

Khwan A Thai term meaning "spirit." In Thai Buddhism every individual possesses 32 *khwan* or spirits.

Kyanzittha The grandson of the founder of the Pagan dynasty in Burma and one of its most powerful rulers. He became king in 1084 A.D.

Lalitavistara A proto-Mahāyāṇa biography of the Buddha.

Liṇga A symbol of the Hindu god, Śiva. Taken by some scholars to be a symbol of the god-king (*devarājā*).

Loi Krathong The festival of the floating (*loi*) boats (*krathong*) celebrated in Thailand during the month of November and thought to be Brahmanical in origin.

Lokeśvara/Avalokiteśvara A *bodhisattva* in deity form whose face dominates the Bayon, the central temple of the ancient Khmer capital of Angkor Thom where it is thought he is identified with the ruler, Jayavarman VII.

Lokiya Literally, "mundane or of the world."

Lokuttara Literally, 'trans-mundane."

Mahākassapa One of the principal disciples of the Buddha.

Mahāparinibbāna Sutta The "Discourse of the Great Decease" which recounts the last days of the Buddha.

Mahāvihāra One of the principal monasteries in the ancient Sinhalese capital of Anurādhapura. The defender of the orthodox Theravada tradition which became normative in Southeast Asia in the thirteenth and fourteenth centuries.

Mahāsammata A ruler of "great justice." A term applied to the first monarch chosen to establish order in a chaotic world (see *Aggañña Suttanta*).

Mahāvamsa "The Great Chronicle," probably the most celebrated chronicle of Sinhalese Buddhism.

Mākha Pūjā The celebration which marks the miraculous gathering of 1250 disciples of the Buddha at Veluvana Mahāvihāra in Rājāgṛha, north India.

Maṇḍala	A diagram usually in the form of a squared circle which in various ways symbolizes the unity of the individual, society and the cosmos. In Southeast Asia ancient capitals, royal and religious buildings were constructed in the form of a *maṇḍala*.
Mañjuśri	In Mahāyāṇa Buddhism the *bodhisattva* of wisdom.
Mantra	A word or chant thought to have special power or potency.
Māra	In the Theravāda tradition the equivalent of Satan.
Moggalāna	One of the Buddha's chief disciples. Frequently he will be depicted paying respects to the Buddha.
Mudrā	A hand position of a Buddha image or a practitioner. In the Theravāda tradition Buddha images are often known by their *mudrās*.
Nat	A Burmese term for a powerful guardian spirit.
Nibbāna (Sanskrit, *Nirvāṇa*)	The soteriological goal in Theravāda Buddhism, meaning to have the passions extinguished, to have gained knowledge into the true nature of things.
Pacceka Buddha	One who becomes a Buddha by his own efforts and who does not share the fruits of his enlightenment with others.
Pāli	The canonical language of Theravāda Buddhism.
Pāramitā	Literally, "perfection." In Theravāda Buddhism the term refers to the ten moral perfections personified in the last ten *jātaka* stories in the Pāli canon., e.g., generosity, compassion.
Paritta	Literally, "protection, safeguard." Came to be applied to a group of texts chanted at auspicious occasions.
Paṭicca-samuppāda	Literally, "dependent co-arising." The term refers to the basic teaching of canonical Theravāda Buddhism which appears in a classical twelve-fold formula.
Pātimokkha	Refers to the 227 rules to which fully ordained monks subscribe in a ceremony of confessional held fortnightly.
Pegu	An ancient Mon cultural, political and religious center in central Burma.
Pathamasambodhi	A text thought to have been written in northern Thailand which recounts the life of the Buddha.
Phī	A Thai term for spirits thought to have malicious or mischievous powers.
Phra Malai	A Thai Buddhist text about a saintly monk who was given the opportunity to see those punished in hell for breaking the Buddhist precepts and rewarded in heaven for keeping them.
Pretaloka	The *pretas* (Sanskrit) are "hungry ghosts." The *pretaloka* refers to one of the hells or places of punishment in the Theravāda cosmology.
Pūjā	To make an offering, to worship, to hold a celebration.
Puñña	Meritorious acts which cause or influence good consequences.

Sama	One of the last ten *jātaka* stories in the Theravāda canon which personifies the virtue of loving kindness.
Samantrabhadra	One of the Mahāyāṇa *bodhisattvas*.
Saṁsāra	Literally, to come again and again, revolve, hence, rebirth or transmigration.
Sāriputta	One of the principal disciples of the Buddha often depicted along with Moggalana paying respects to the Buddha.
Sarvodāya Shramadāna	An organization dedicated to social service and rural uplift based on Buddhist principles. Founded by A.T. Ariyaratne in Sri Lanka.
Sigālovāda Sutta	One of the discourses in the *Dīgha Nikāya* (Long Discourses) which lays out what is often referred to as the "ethic of the householder."
Sīla	Moral virtue. Often thought of in terms of the basic Buddhist precepts, i.e., not to kill, steal, lie, etc.
Sīmā	The boundary stones which set off monastic precincts or an ordination hall.
Śiva	One of the principal Hindu gods who plays varying roles in different Theravāda cultural traditions.
Stūpa	A Sanskrit term designating a sepulchral mound or monument, e.g., the Sāñcī Stūpa.
Suddhodana	The father of the Buddha.
Sumeru, Mt.	In Indian cosmology the central axis or mountain of the universe.
Suññata	Literally, "emptiness."
Sutta	Literally, "thread." Comes to stand for threads of discourse or dialogue texts in the Pāli canon of Theravāda Buddhism.
Tathāgata	A title of the Buddha. Refers to his "crossing over" to Nibbāna, i.e., his enlightenment. Literally, "thus-come."
Tavatiṁsa	One of the heavens in the Theravāda cosmology. The Buddha is reputed to have preached the *Abhidhamma* there to his mother.
Tilokarāja (1442-1487)	Probably the greatest Buddhist monarch of northern Thailand.
Upasampadā	Higher ordination or ordination into the Buddhist monkhood.
Upekkhā	Equanimity. One of the "sublime states."
Uposatha	The Buddhist sabbath days which are calculated according to the four phases of the moon.
Uruvelā	An important town in northern India during the lifetime of the Buddha.
Vairocana	"Illumination." The Buddha in his transcendental aspect.
Vajrasattva	Literally, a "diamond being." A term in the Varjayāṇa tradition for a fully realized being.

Vassa	The period of the monsoon rains retreat observed by Buddhist monks, usually between July and October.
Vessantara	The last incarnation of the Buddha prior to his rebirth as Siddhattha Gotama. The last of the *jātaka* stories; a personification of the virtue of generosity.
Vihāra	Literally, "an abode or dwelling place." Also refers to a place where monks gather for services of chanting.
Vinaya	The monk's discipline. The *Vinaya Piṭaka* refers to those texts which deal with the monastic order and the discipline.
Vipassanā	Meditation of the insight rather than the trance variety.
Vīsakhā Pūjā	An occasion celebrating the birth, enlightenment and death of the Buddha. Usually occurs in May.
Viṣṇu	One of the principal Hindu deities. Appears in various guises in different Therāvada cultures.
Yasodhara	The Buddha's wife.